FARNHAM
IN 50 BUILDINGS

PAT DARGAN

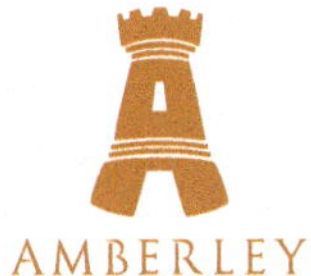

AMBERLEY

First published 2023

Amberley Publishing, The Hill, Stroud
Gloucestershire GL5 4EP

www.amberley-books.com

British Library Cataloguing in Publication Data.
A catalogue record for this book is available from the British Library.

ISBN 978 1 3981 1190 5 (print)
ISBN 978 1 3981 1191 2 (ebook)

Typesetting by SJmagic DESIGN SERVICES, India.
Printed in Great Britain.

Appointed GPSR EU Representative: Easy Access System Europe Oü, 16879218
Address: Mustamäe tee 50, 10621, Tallinn, Estonia
Contact Details: gpsr.requests@easproject.com, +358 40 500 3575

Contents

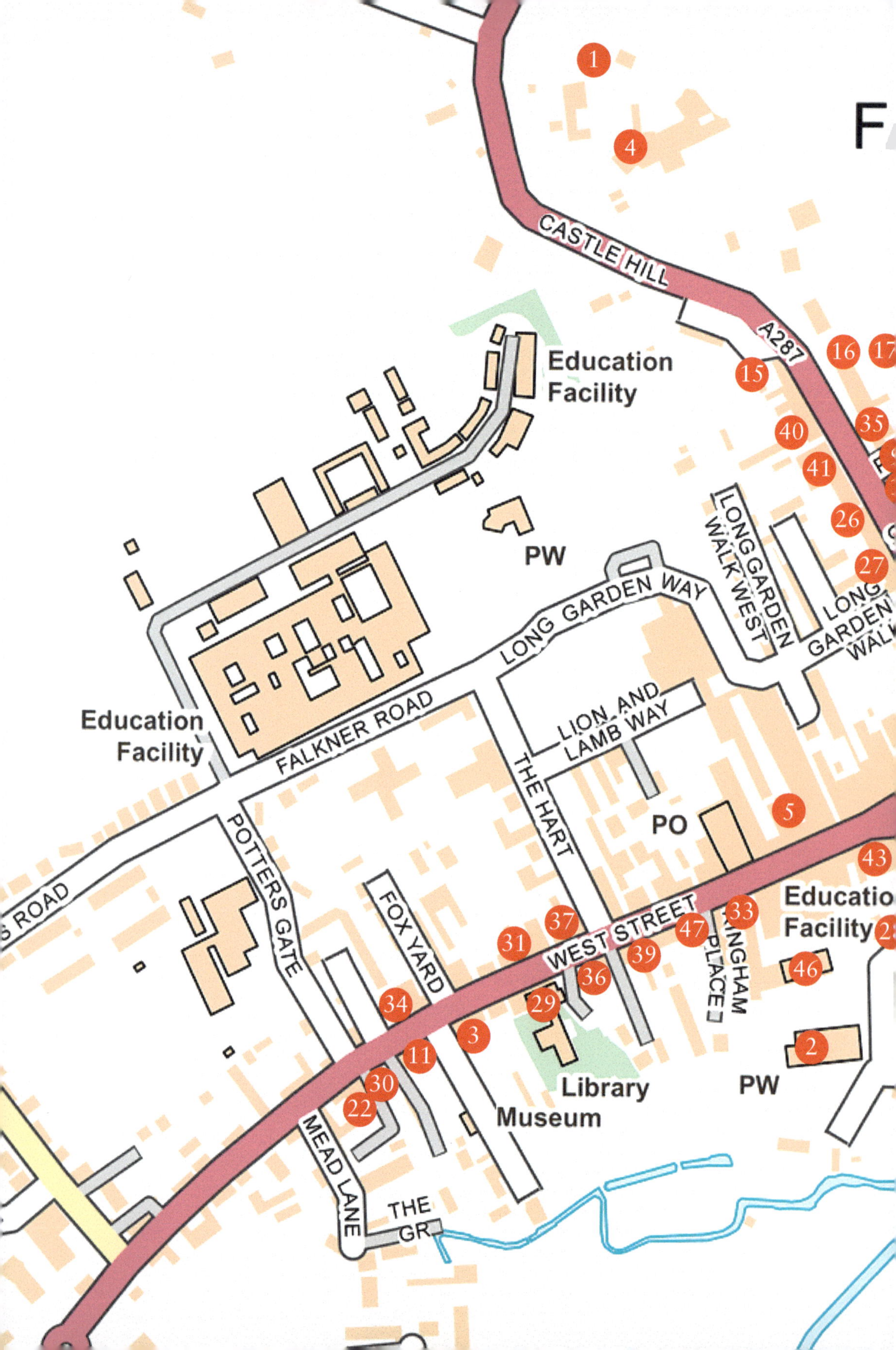

CASTLE HILL
A287
Education Facility
PW
Education Facility
FALKNER ROAD
POTTERS GATE
LONG GARDEN WAY
LONG GARDEN WALK WEST
LONG GARDEN WALK
LION AND LAMB WAY
THE HART
PO
FOX YARD
WEST STREET
Education Facility
GINGHAM PLACE
MEAD LANE
THE GR
Library
Museum
PW
ROAD
F

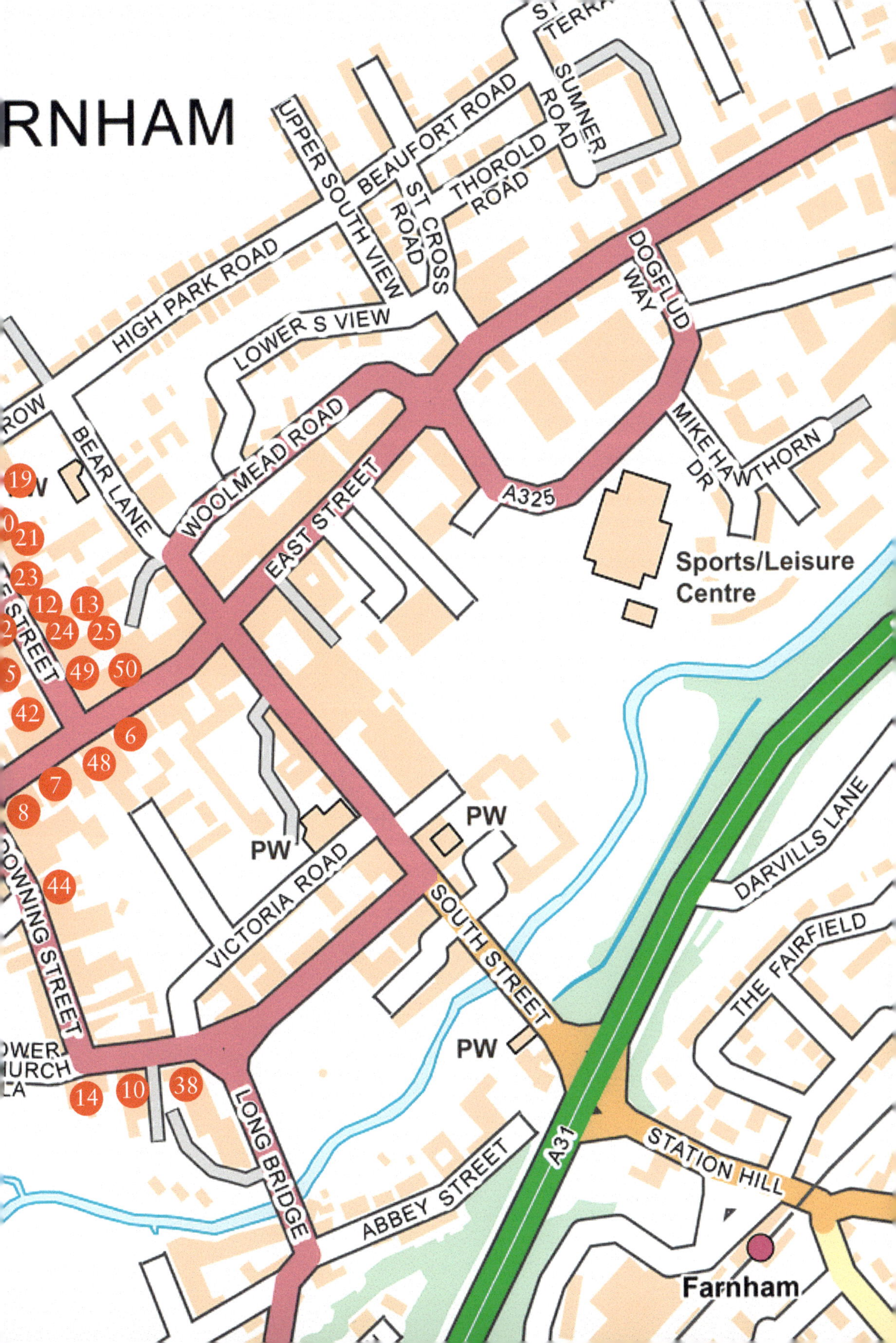

RNHAM
19
0
21
23
12
13
2
24
25
5
49
50
42
6
48
7
8
44
14
10
38
HIGH PARK ROAD
UPPER SOUTH VIEW
BEAR LANE
WOOLMEAD ROAD
LOWER S VIEW
BEAUFORT ROAD
ST CROSS ROAD
THOROLD ROAD
SUMNER ROAD
ST TERRA
EAST STREET
DOGFLUD WAY
MIKE HAWTHORN DR
HAWTHORN
A325
Sports/Leisure Centre
E STREET
ROW
V
DOWNING STREET
OWER CHURCH LA
VICTORIA ROAD
PW
PW
PW
SOUTH STREET
LONG BRIDGE
ABBEY STREET
A31
DARVILLS LANE
THE FAIRFIELD
STATION HILL
Farnham

Key

Introduction

Farham is a market town in Surrey located approximately 35 miles south-west of London and developed in three main historic phases: Saxon, medieval and Georgian. The Saxon origins of the town lie in a seventh-century settlement established on the north bank of the River Wey and came under the control of the Bishop of Winchester around AD 800. Little survives of this early settlement except for the remains of several sixth-century Saxon huts discovered to the south of the current town in 1924. The medieval (Norman) development at Farnham began around 1138 when Bishop Henry de Bois, grandson of William the Conqueror, began work on the building of Farnham Castle on a raised site north of the Saxon area. This was initially a motte-and-bailey earthen fort that included a circular mound with a wooden tower and a surrounding stockade. This provided accommodation for the bishop on his frequent journeys to London.

Later in the twelfth century Bishop Henry strengthened his castle and laid out a formally planned new town on the south side of the castle. This included Castle Street, which extended southwards from the castle gate to link with the east–west alignment of The Borough and resulted in an inverted T-shaped plan that was enclosed by a defensive town ditch, which survives in parts. A little later the boundary of The Borough extended westwards along the line of West Street. Curiously, the earlier Saxon area of the settlement, which was positioned on the south side of West Street, lay outside the new defended area, although it held the parish church of St Andrew. Following this, the town was granted a charter by William de Ralegh, Bishop of Winchester, in 1249 and the three streets were lined by narrow building plots on which timber-framed houses were constructed within the town ditch – in addition to a market house on the corner of Castle Street and The Borough.

During the eighteenth and nineteenth centuries the medieval wooden houses that once lined the streets were gradually removed over time and replaced by Georgian brick houses in a variety of different widths and heights, most of which survive today. An intriguing aspect of some of these Georgian houses is that they were superimposed on the wooden framework of the earlier medieval buildings – a feature not easily observable. The result is a Georgian core of vibrant housing of outstanding richness and local history that includes Castle Street, The Borough, West Street, and Downing Street – the latter providing a dogleg access from West Street to the medieval St Andrew's Parish Church. From this historic core, fifty buildings have been selected and presented here in the chronological sequence in which they appeared and which, in the writer's view, highlight and represent the best of Farnham's architectural heritage.

During the following late nineteenth and twentieth centuries the fabric of Farnham continued to expand outwards beyond the historic core, notably westwards and eastward in a complex arrangement of housing, administrative and institutional buildings in Victorian and modern building styles.

The 50 Buildings

Farnham Castle dates from around 1297 when it was laid out by Bishop Henry de Blois, on a hilltop site overlooking the Saxon town of Farnham. The initial castle structure took the form of a high earth-built motte-and-bailey structure

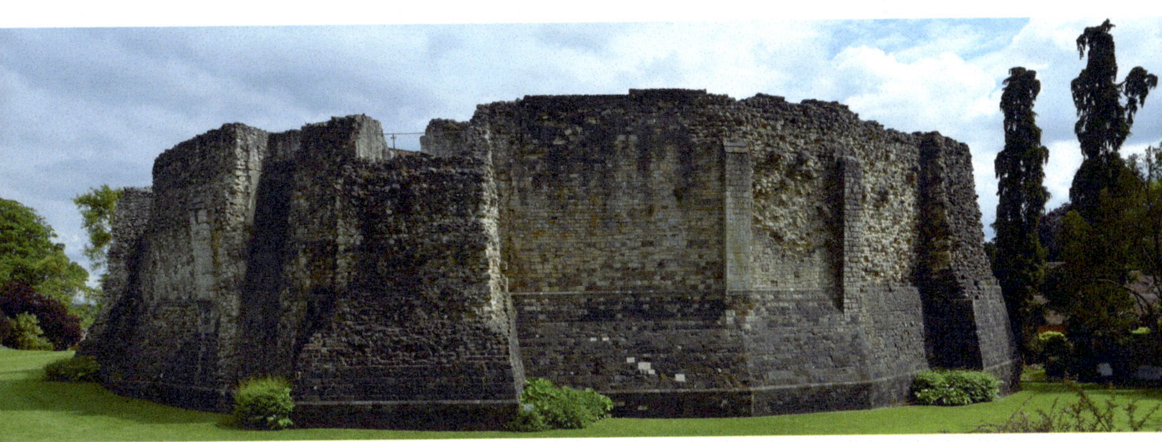

Above: Farnham Castle keep. (Courtesy of Lewis Hulbert, CC BY-SA 3.0)

Right: The partially ruined gatehouse and approach to Farnham Castle.

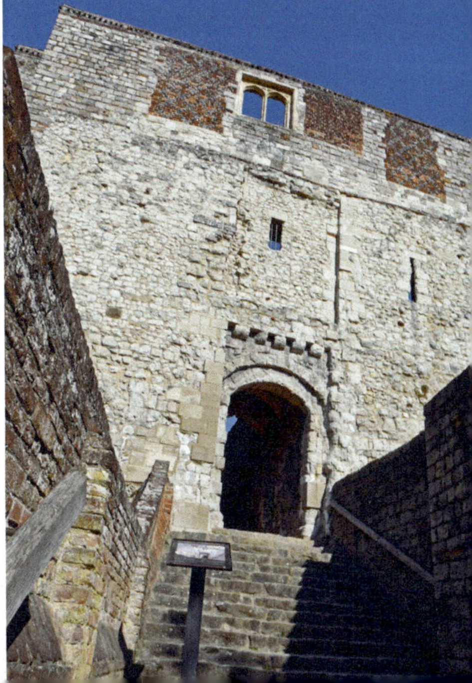

with a central mound enclosed by a wooden circular stockade – a form of defence structure frequently built by the Normans all across the British Isles. A short time later the stockade was removed and replaced by a stone curtain wall that established an oval bastion with a rectangular tower on one side. Around 1470 Bishop Fox added a three-storey gatehouse with a mixture of stonework and diaper-patterned brickwork, now mostly in a ruined condition, in addition to stone entrance steps and a drawbridge. On the south side of the castle a group of later buildings, including the fifteenth-century stables (see No. 4, p. 14), were arranged in a cluster around a triangular outer courtyard.

2. St Andrew's Church, Upper Church Lane, Twelfth Century

The parish church of St Andrew in Upper Church Lane dates from the twelfth century and replaced an earlier Saxon church, the remains of which were uncovered during recent architectural excavations. The layout of the church consisted initially of a cruciform plan with a central nave, chancel and a north and south transept. During the fourteenth and fifteenth centuries a north and south side aisles were added to the nave, which included St George's Chapel on the north side and the

St Andrew's Church. (© Copyright Stefan Czapski, CC BY-SA 2.0)

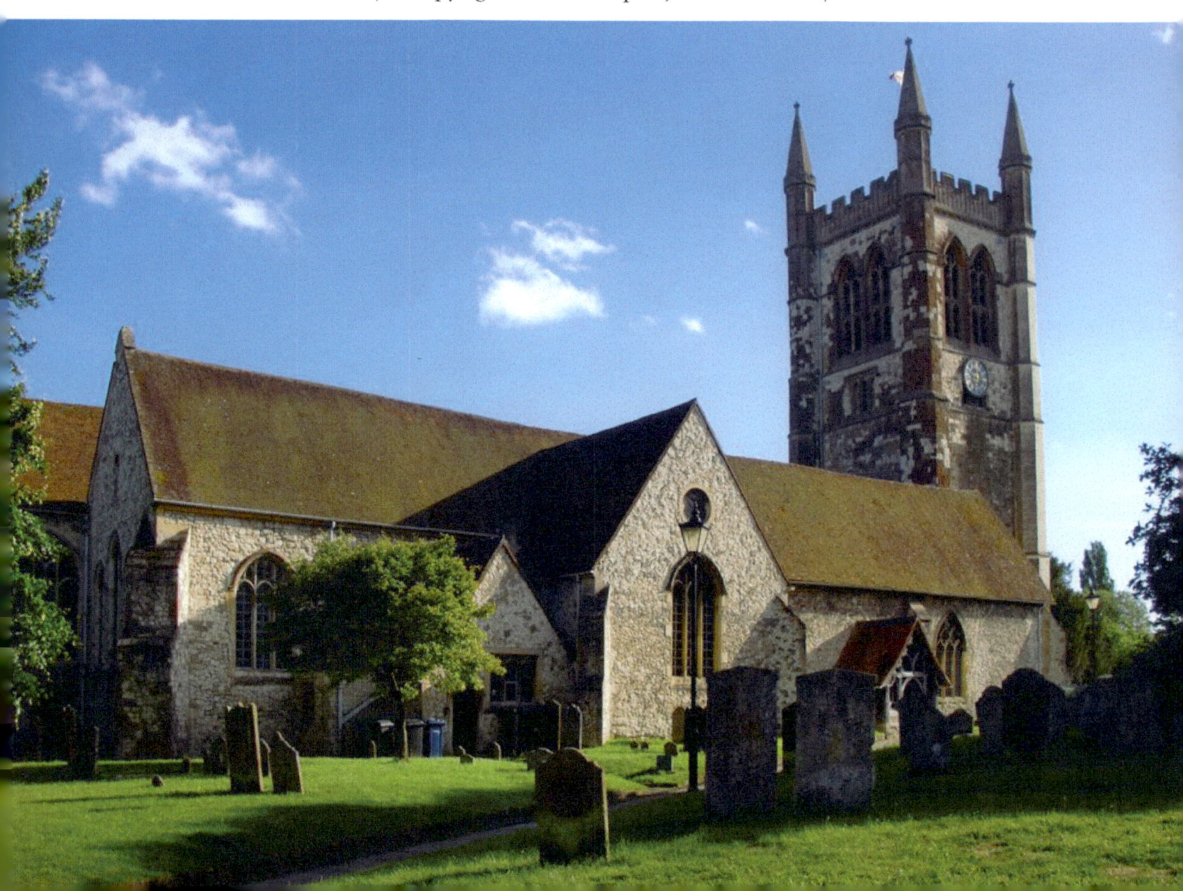

Lady Chapel on the south side, in addition to which an entrance porch was added to north side of the church. Later, in the sixteenth century, a tower was added to west end of the nave and during the nineteenth century a vestry was attached to the end of the north transept in addition to a small extension to the south transept.

Externally, the church features a range of characteristic Gothic features including heavy stone walling, steep gables, corner turrets, slated roofs, pointed door and window openings, and a tall tower. The pattern of windows varies from slim lancets to wide and elaborate examples of tracery with moulded surrounds and elaborated with stained-glass working. The west elevation has three pronounced gabled bays, representing the three rooflines of the nave and side aisles, each with a tall individual Gothic window with hood moulding, intricate tracery and stained glass. The tall square church tower on the west gable has pointed windows, pinnacle-topped corner buttresses, and battlements. This was built in the sixteenth century and was raised to its present height around 1865. Internally the nave is separated from the side aisles by arcades of moulded arched carried on plain chamfered square columns, in addition to a rich arrangement of burial and memorial wall plaques. Overhead the roof of the nave features hammerbeam roof trusses and painted wooden ceilings, while the side aisles have crown post or triangular-framed roof trusses.

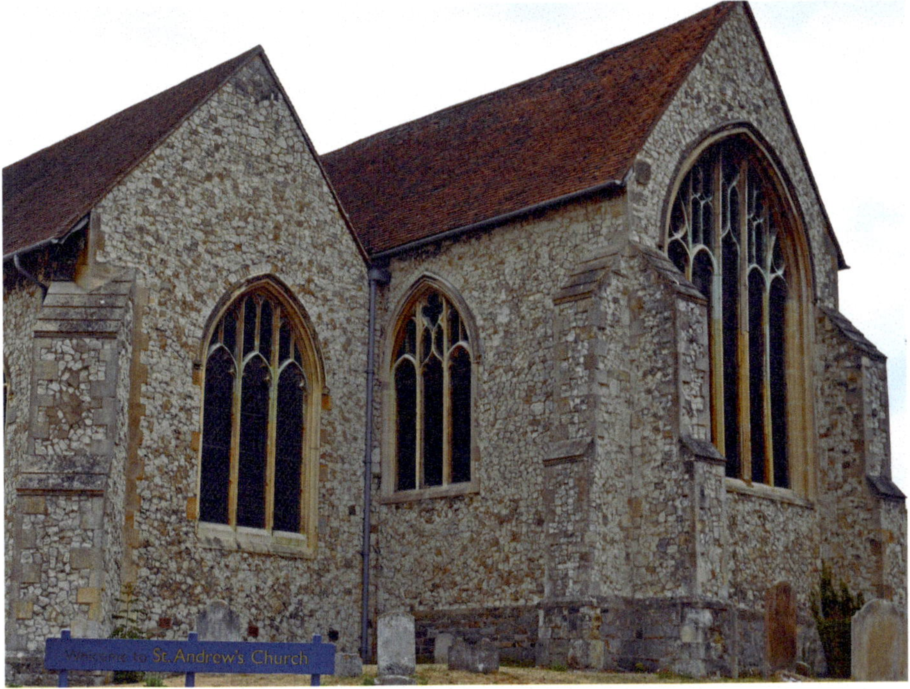

The elevations of St Andrew's Church display many of the characteristic elements of Gothic architecture, including heavy masonry walling, steep gables, a tower, as well as pointed-arched window and door openings.

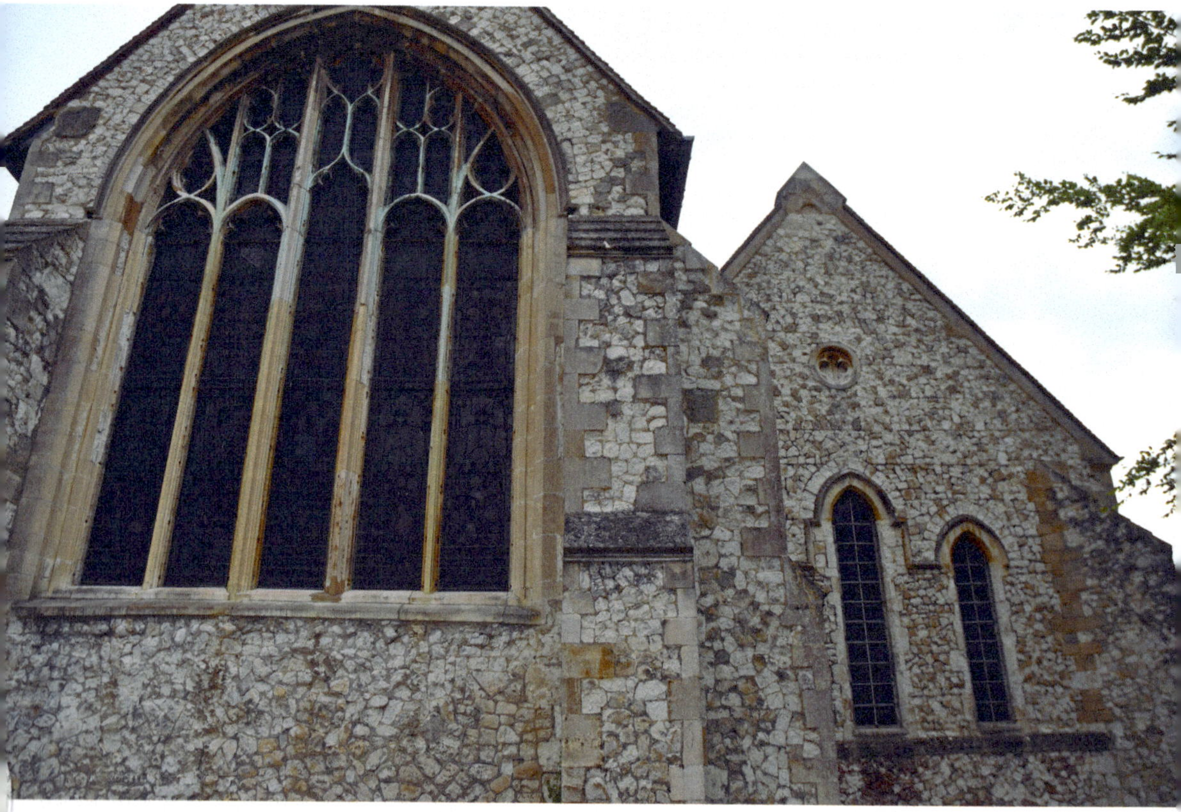

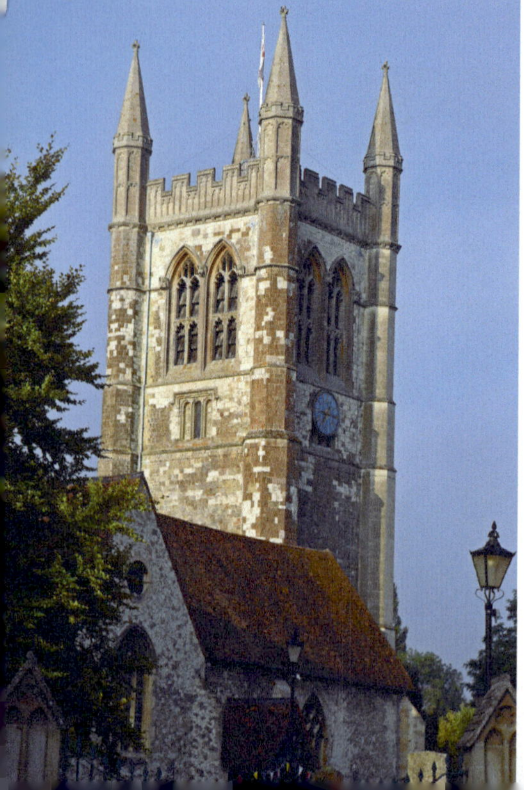

Above: The west elevation of St Andrew's Church has triple gables, each featuring corner buttresses and a tall Gothic window with elaborate tracery.

Left: The square tower of St Andrew's Church extends well above the roof, with pointed windows, pinnacle-topped corner buttresses, and battlements.

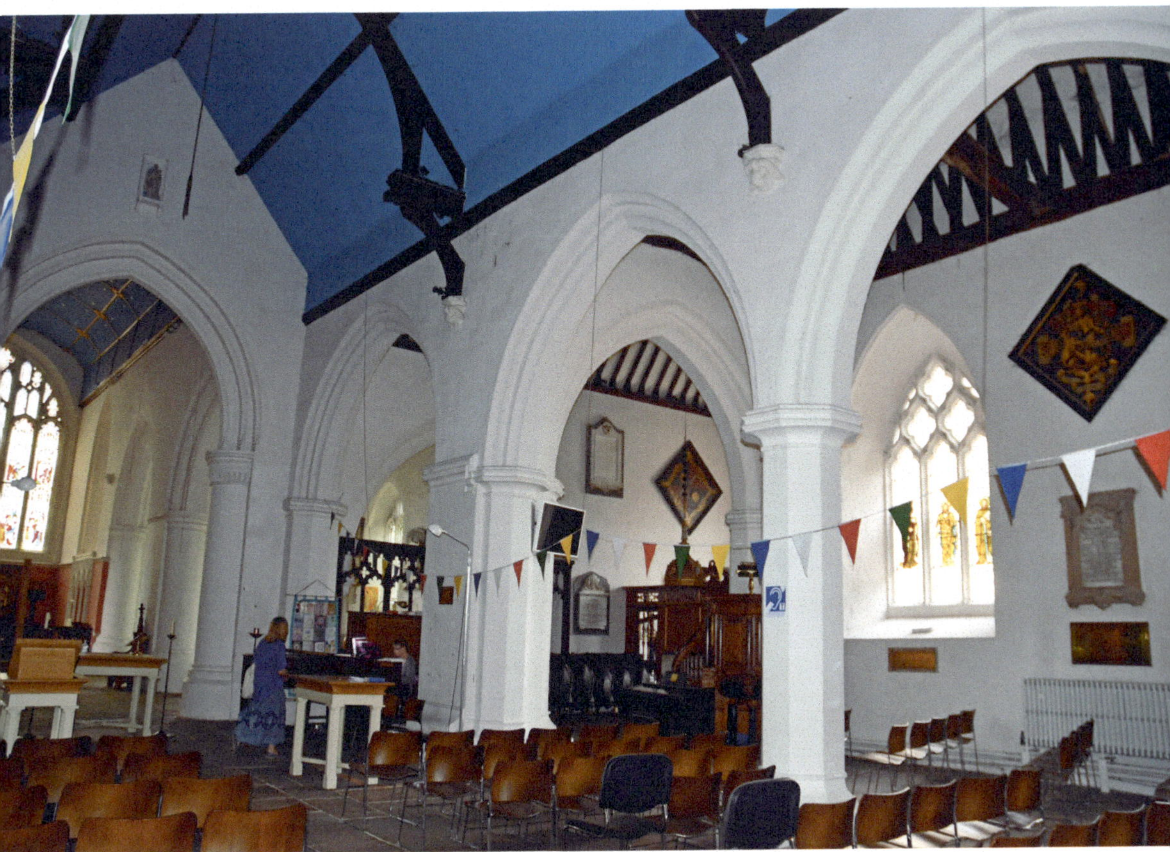

The nave of St Andrew's Church is separated from the side aisles and transepts by arcades of wide, pointed arches with slim columns.

3. Hall House, West Street, Fourteenth Century

The two-storey house on West Street, once known as Timber Hall, has a hipped roof, white-painted brickwork and is currently divided into a number of independent houses. The date of the building is uncertain, but it displays a number of distinguishing features suggestive of a fourteenth century hall house that was subsequently divided into three separate dwellings. These include a wide frontage, a tiled hipped roof, roof space accommodation, and a street facing projecting gabled bay at one end. The building also features other elements, perhaps from the eighteenth century or later. The ground floor has two entrance doorways, and four camber-headed windows with a mixed arrangement of sliding and leaded casement sashes; while the first floor has two half dormer windows with leaded sashes and a single sliding sash window on the gable.

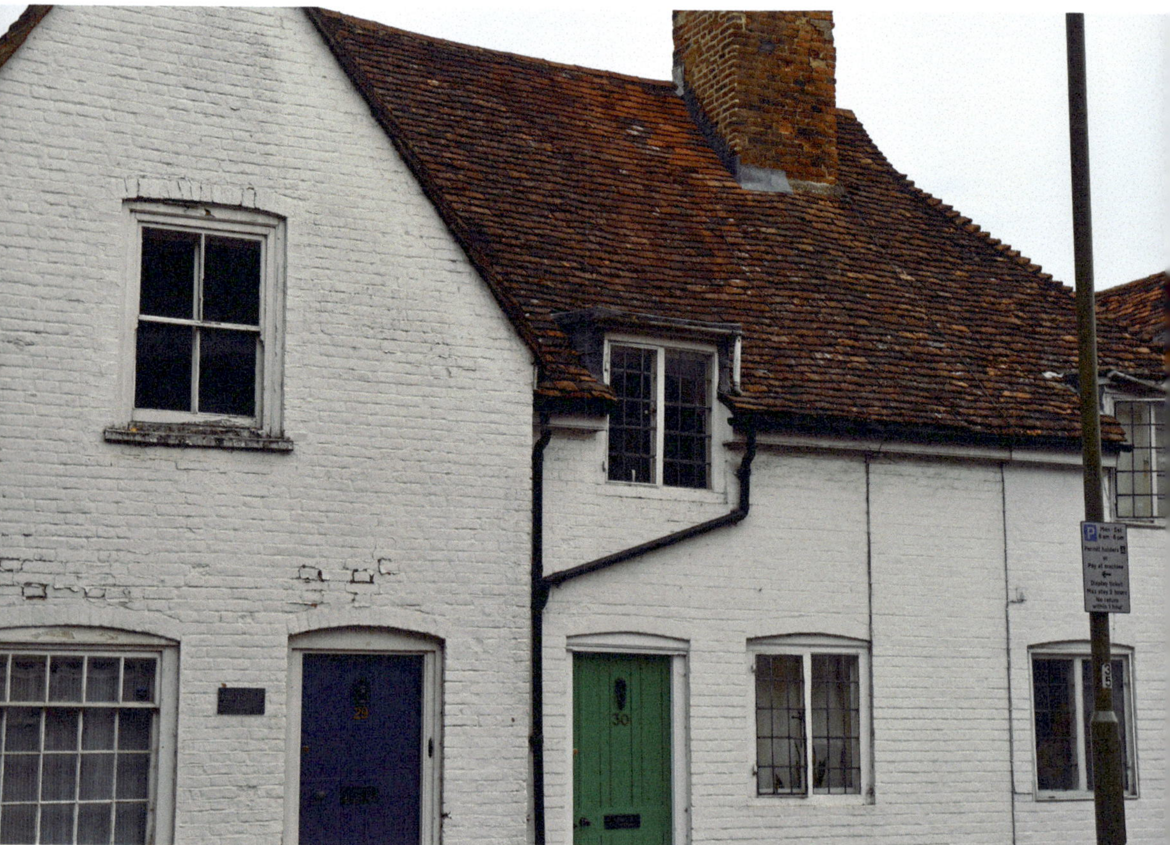

The probable hall house on West Street has a tiled, hipped roof and a projecting street-facing gable at one end.

4. Fox's Tower, Farnham Castle, 1470–75

Fox's Tower stable building is one of a cluster of buildings, of various dates, that enclose the triangular courtyard on the south side of Farnham Castle keep. This is a tall three-storey square tower with herringbone brickwork and a projecting corner tower. The main tower has an irregular arrangement of Georgian windows on all fronts and a brick parapet that includes projecting corbels and stepped battlements. The south elevation has an arched entrance on one side with two windows on each of the first and second floors overhead, in addition to a painted sundial above the arch. On the far corner of the elevation is a projecting tower with splayed corners, the height of which extends above the main parapet line, marking it as one of the main features of the complex. This has three windows, one above the other at each of the floor levels on one side, as well as a painted sundial on the blank splayed face. There is a similar but simpler tower adjacent to the archway.

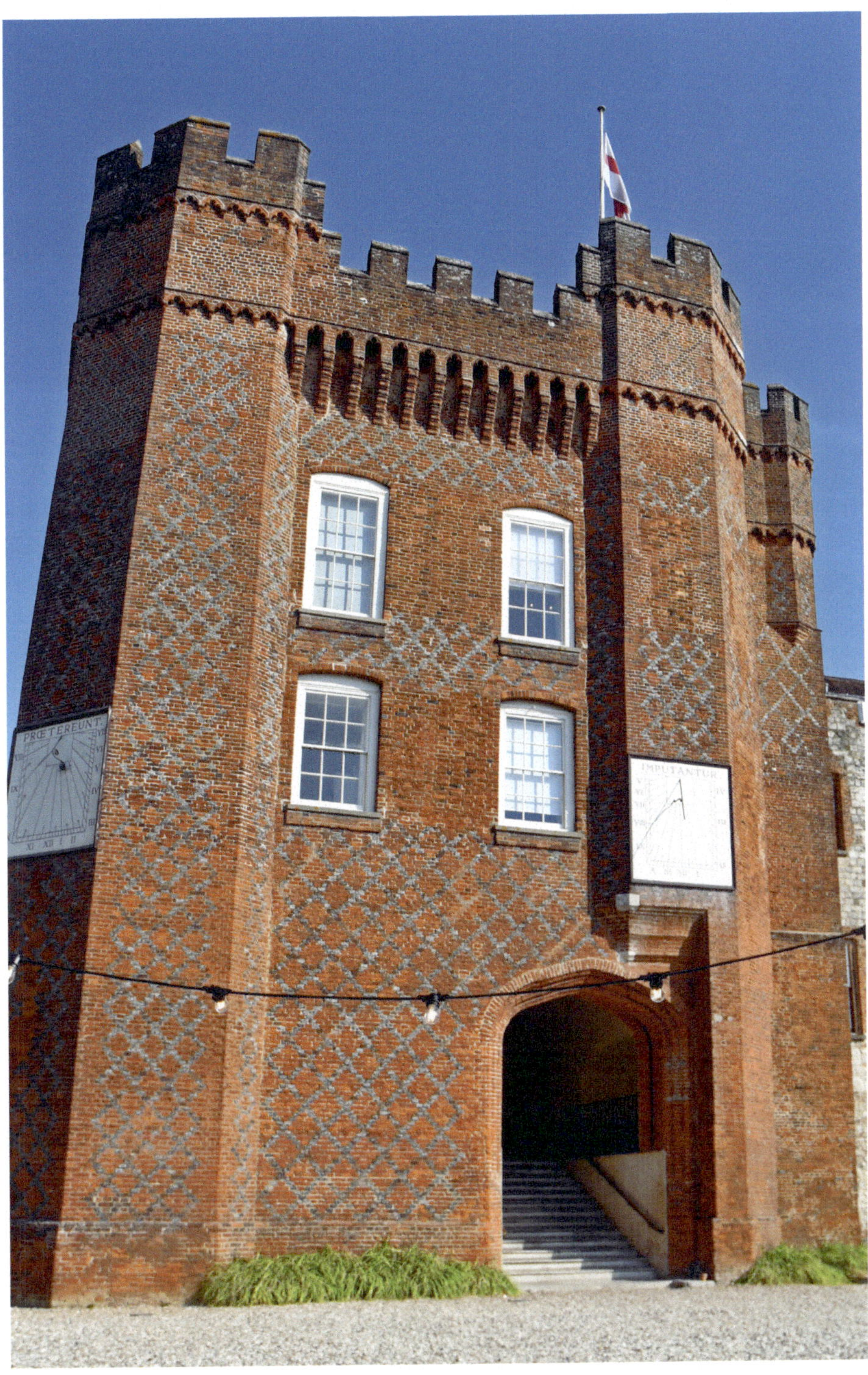

Fox's Tower, to the south of Farnham Castle, is a tall, three-storey tower with herringbone brickwork, a corner tower and brick battlements.

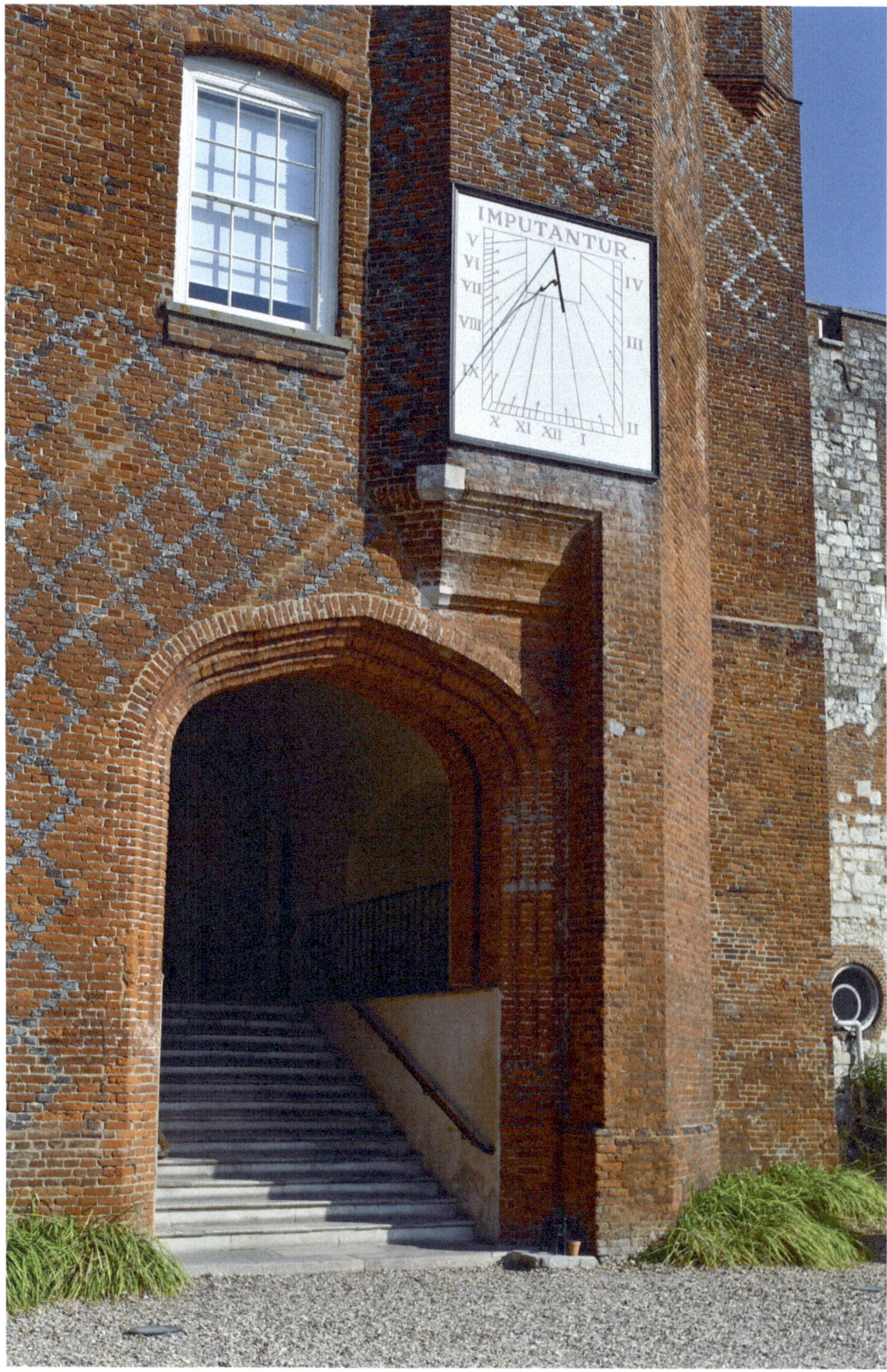

The south elevation of Fox's Tower, south of Farnham Castle, has an arched entrance to one side and painted sundial above.

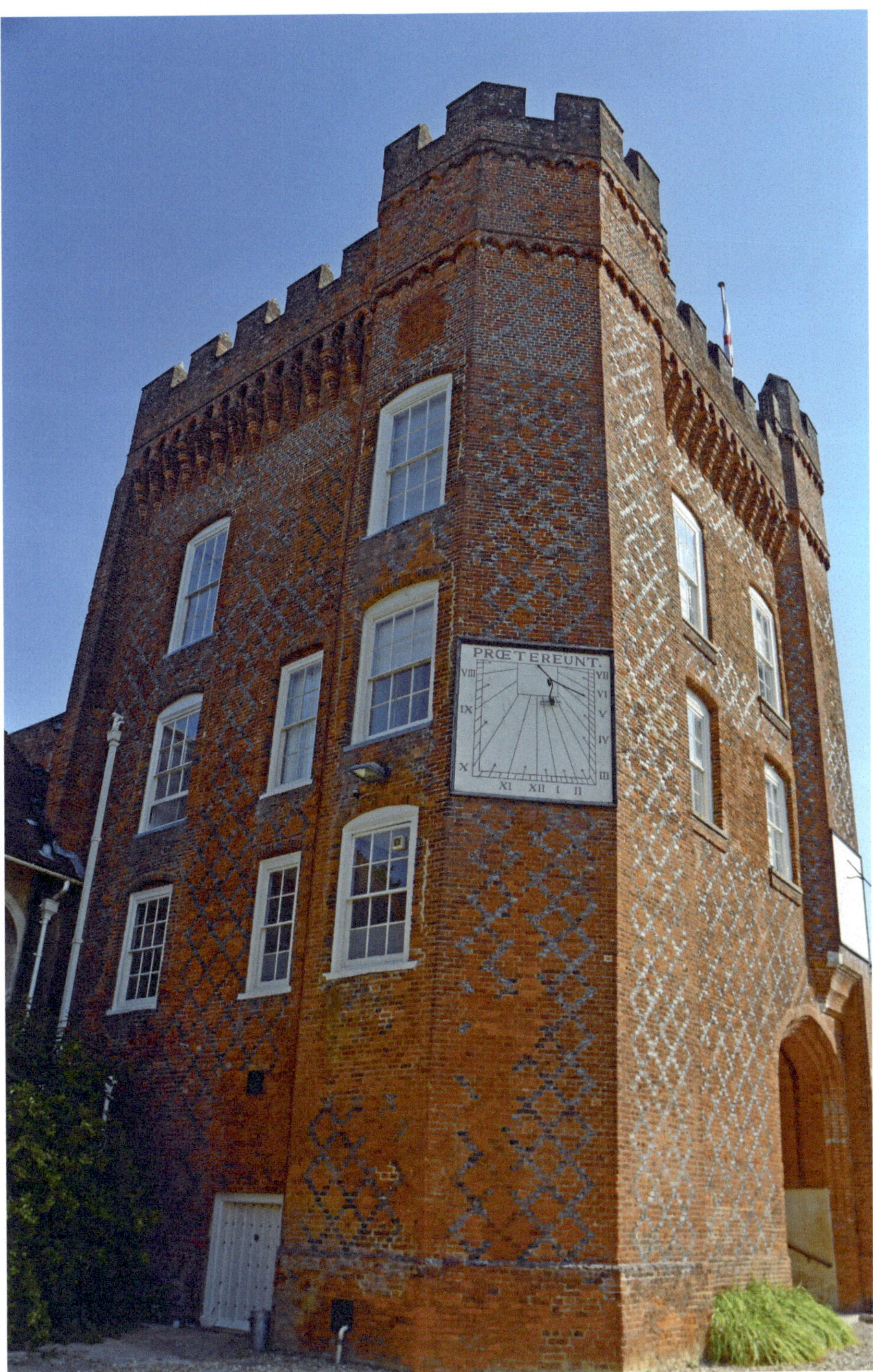

The corner tower of Fox's Tower is splayed with a painted sundial on the blank face.

5. Former Lion and Lamb Inn, West Street, 1537

The former Lion and Lamb Coaching Inn dates from 1537 according to the brick date panel on the inner wall of the entrance arch. The original building was demolished around 1910 and rebuilt during the 1930s. The current building is two storeys high with an extended street elevation and a central gabled bay. The ground level features three recent shopfronts, each with a glazed shop door

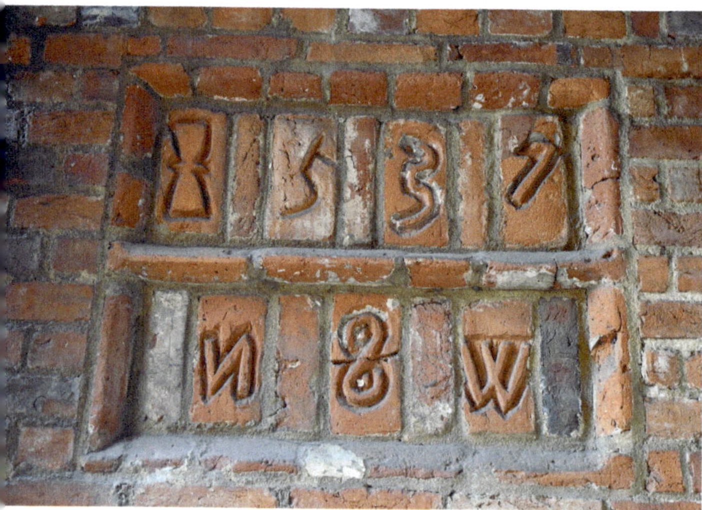

Left: The 1537 date stone on the entrance archway to the former Lion and Lamb Inn, West Street.

Below: The street elevation of the former Lion and Lamb Inn, West Street.

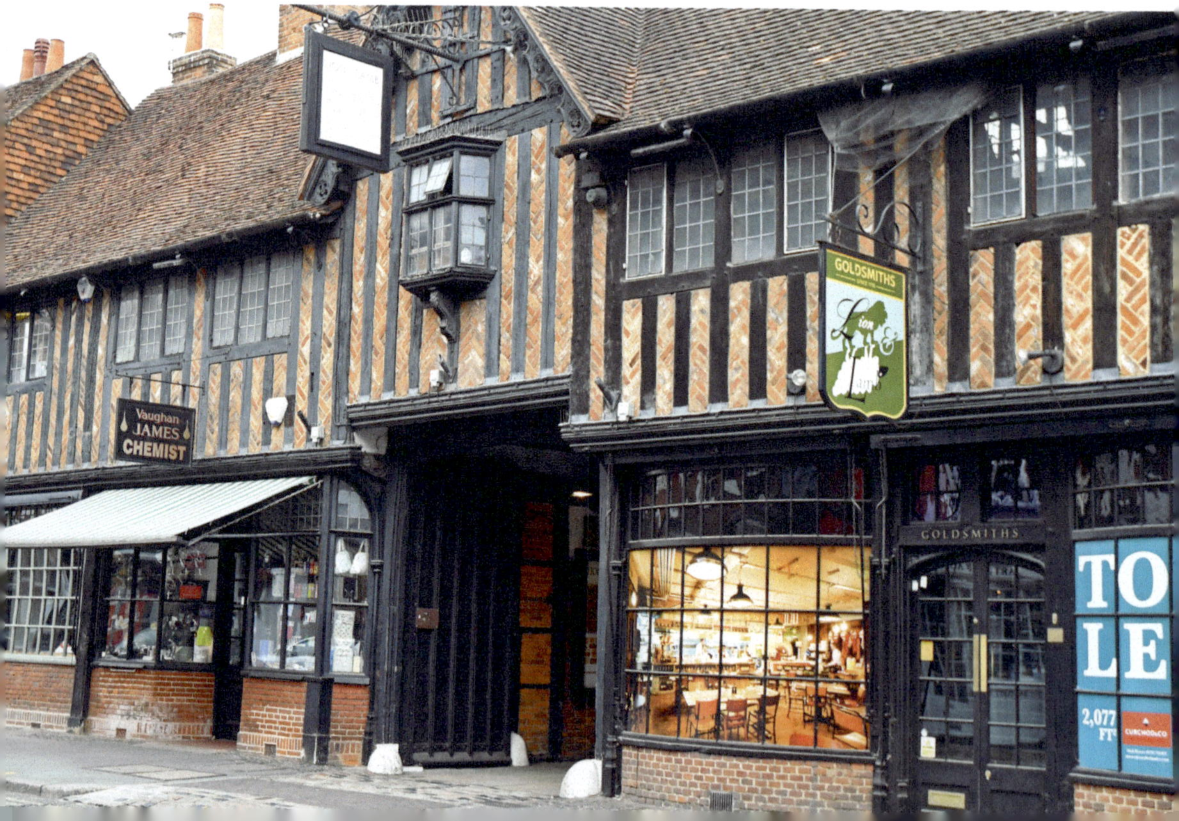

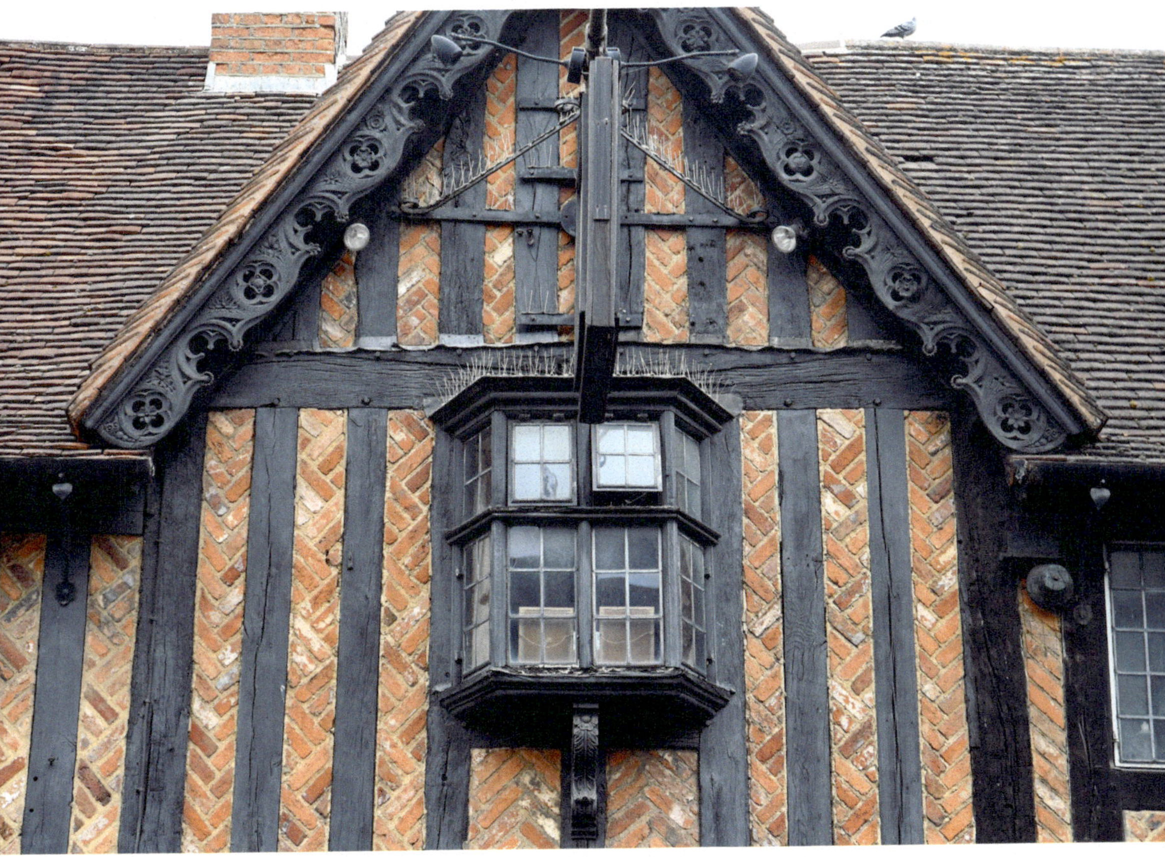

The overhead gabled central bay of the former Lion and Lamb Inn, West Street.

and display windows with small pane glazing. The central bay has a flat arch rectangular opening with sheeted doors that provides access to recently completed commercial developments at the rear. The first floor has a pattern of herringbone brickwork spaced between narrow vertical timber framing and five leaded casement windows spaced across the front. The central bay projects slightly forward and has a similar herringbone brickwork pattern with a small central angled oriel window and ornate bargeboards. Overhead, the tiled roof extends across the full width of the building.

6. Tudor-style Framed Building and Shop, The Borough, Seventeenth Century

The timber-framed house and shop on The Borough is one of three adjacent Tudor-style buildings here. This dates from around the seventeenth century and is two storeys high with an attic storey. The shopfront on the ground level dates from the twentieth century and features a central glazed double door and two plain large

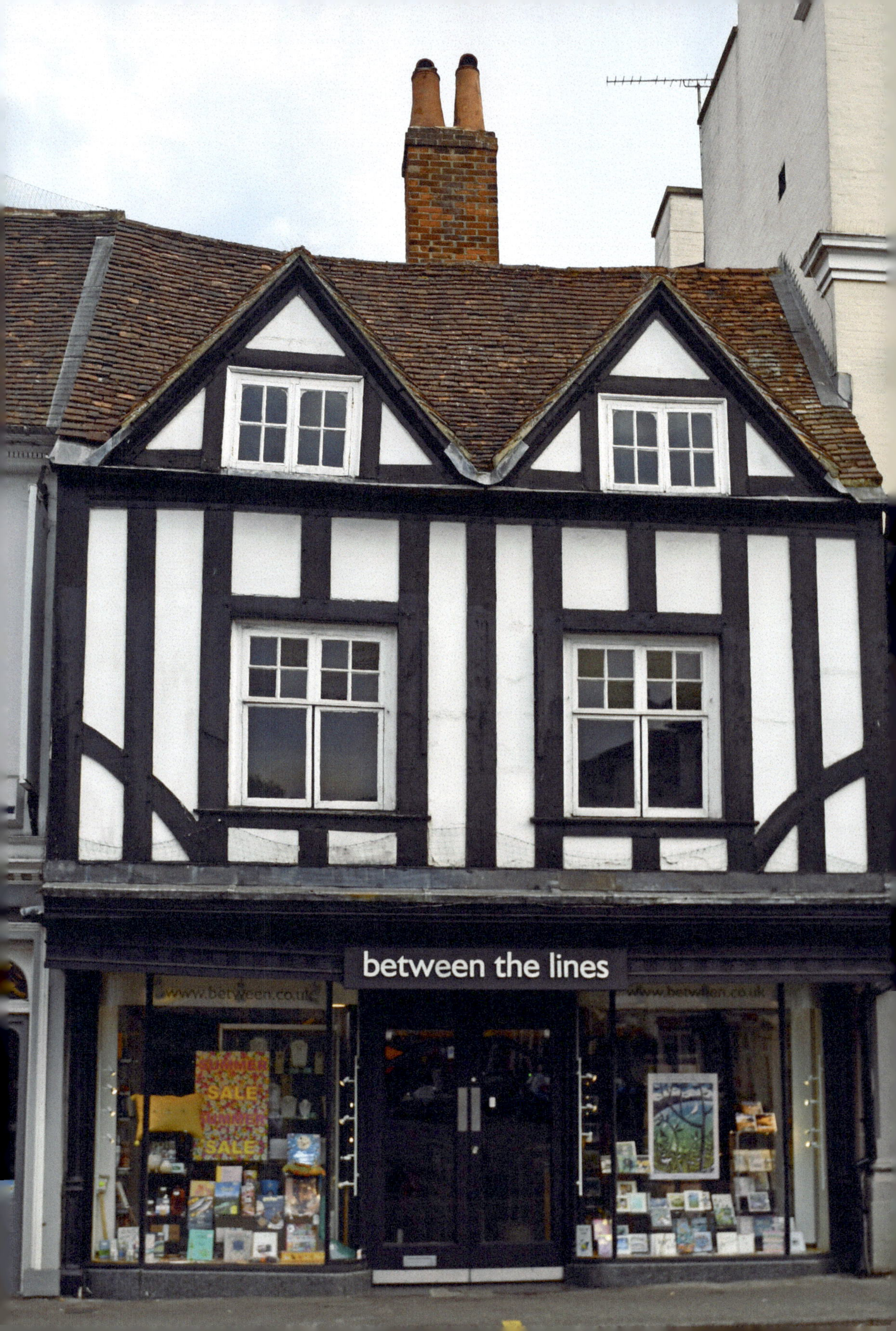

www.between.co.uk
between the lines
www.between.co.uk
SUMMER
SALE
SUMMER
SALE

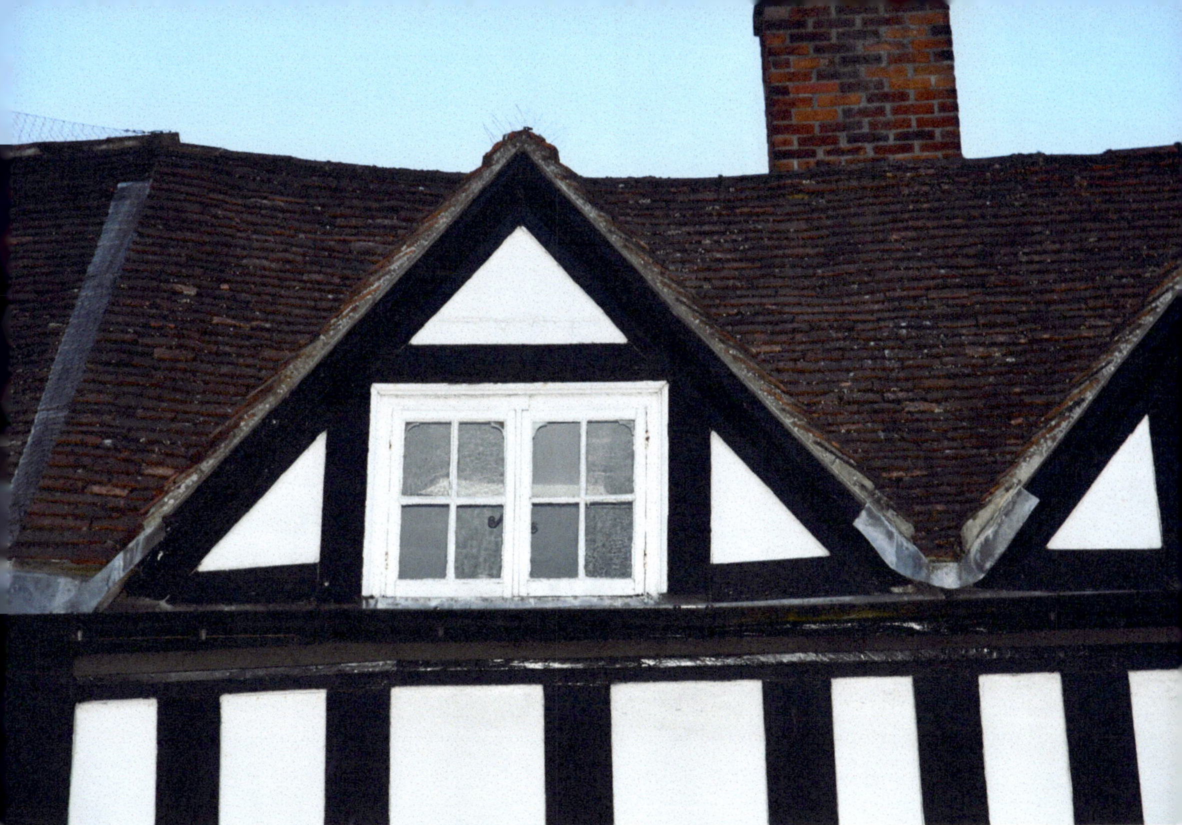

Above: The casement attic window and gable of the house and shop, The Borough.

Opposite: The double-storey Tudor-style timber-framed house and shop on The Borough.

flanking display windows, with a moulded entablature, or crossbeam, overhead. The first-floor level features wooden framing with stucco infilling and a pair of casement windows with small and large panes evenly spaced across the front. The roof is tiled and has two gabled attic windows with small pane casements.

7. Spinning Wheel, The Borough, Sixteenth Century

The Tudor-style three-storey wooden-framed Spinning Wheel building on The Borough dates from around the sixteenth century. This has a double-gable front divided into a complex arrangement of framed panels, on all levels, mostly with curved diagonal bracing. Each floor jetties, or over sails, the one beneath. The building probably acted as a merchant's house and was subsequently used as a post office before being used as an inn. The ground floor of the building has a wide entrance to the yards at the rear. To the right of this a Georgian-style shopfront has recently been inserted. This includes an entrance to the left-hand side of the shopfront, a curved display window and a plain display section – both with multiple square glazing panes. Above the shopfront is an extended window arrangement of leaded windows, including a central projecting bay. The first-floor

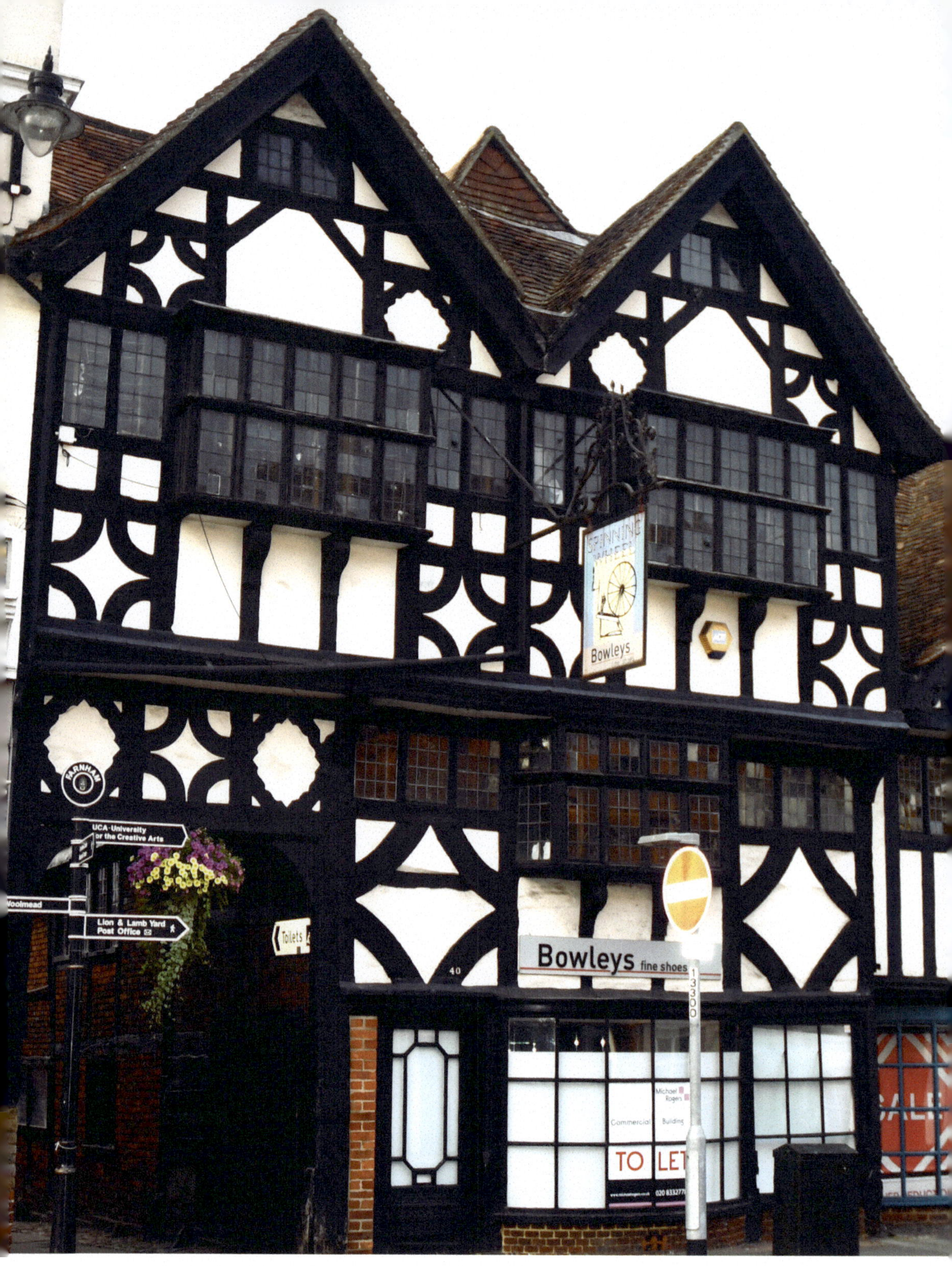

The Tudor-style Spinning Wheel building on The Borough has a complex arrangement of jettied floor levels, framed panels and leaded windows.

level has a run of small-pane leaded windows that stretch across the front, which includes two projecting bays each with ten leaded panes. The overhead third-floor level sits immediately below the twin gables and, in addition to the panels, has a pair of small casement leaded attic windows. Above this, the roof tiling projects over the triangular arrange barge boards.

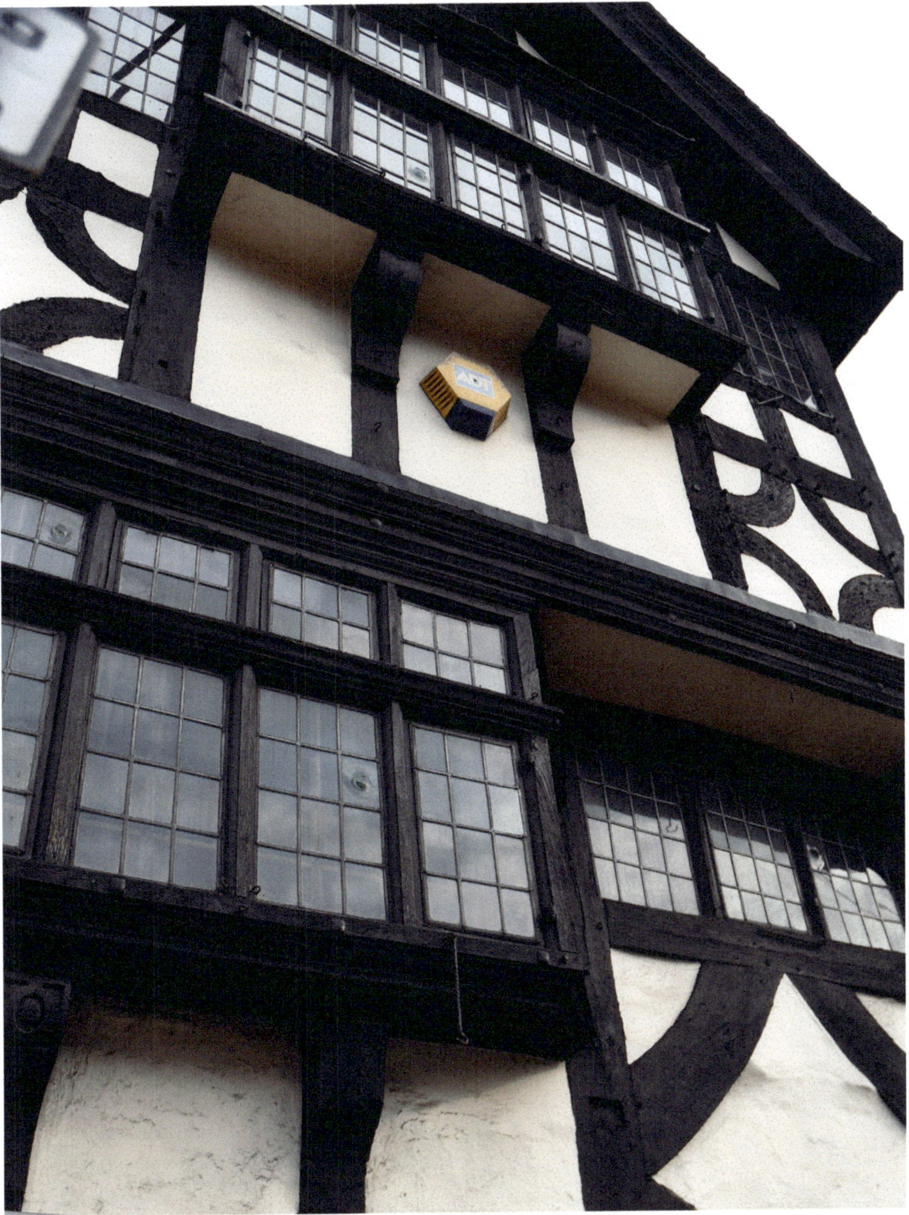

The timber framing, diagonal bracing and leaded widow of the Spinning Wheel on The Borough.

8. Tudor-style Framed Building and Shop, The Borough, Sixteenth Century

The timber-framed Tudor-style building on The Borough dates from around the sixteenth century and was rebuilt around 1930. The timber-framed house is three storeys high with a tiled roof and single gable on the top level. The shopfront on the ground floor of the house has recently been added and has a central shop door flanked on both sides with display windows. These have bays with multiple Georgian-style panes. Above this the two upper-floor levels are jettied, or projected, slightly forward – one above the other. The first-floor level has narrow vertical framing with stucco infilling, four different-sized leaded casement windows and central leaded oriel, or projecting, window with splayed sides and mullioned and transom frames. The upper-level triangular gable has close spaced vertical framing with stucco infilling and a central leaded casement window. The panelling also has diagonal bracing at the apex and the angled bargeboards have carved decorations.

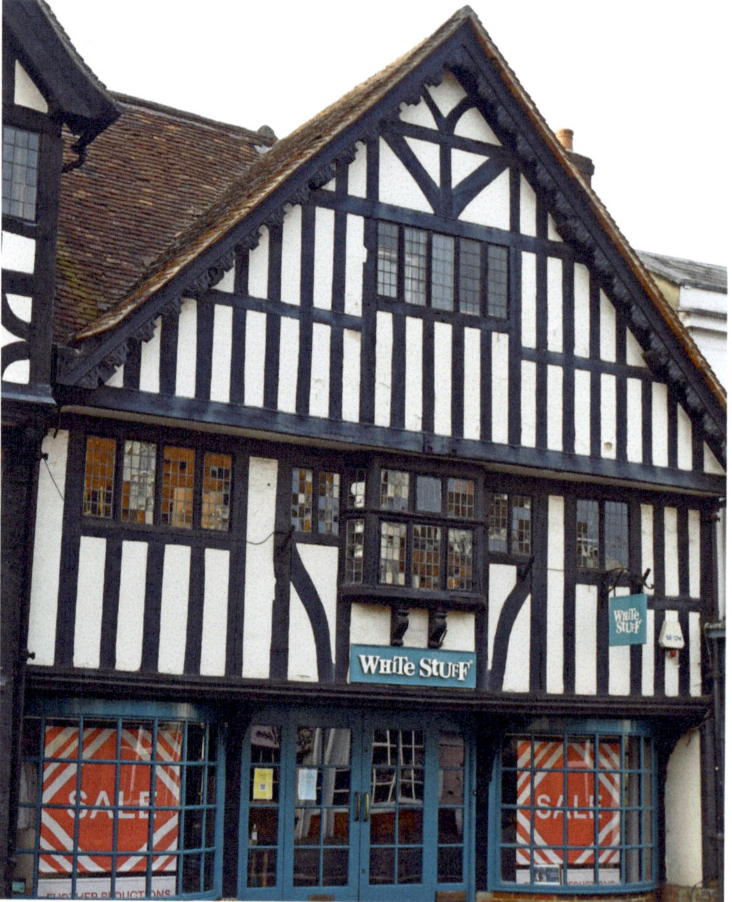

The Tudor-style timber-framed house and shop on The Borough is three storeys high with a single gable on the upper level.

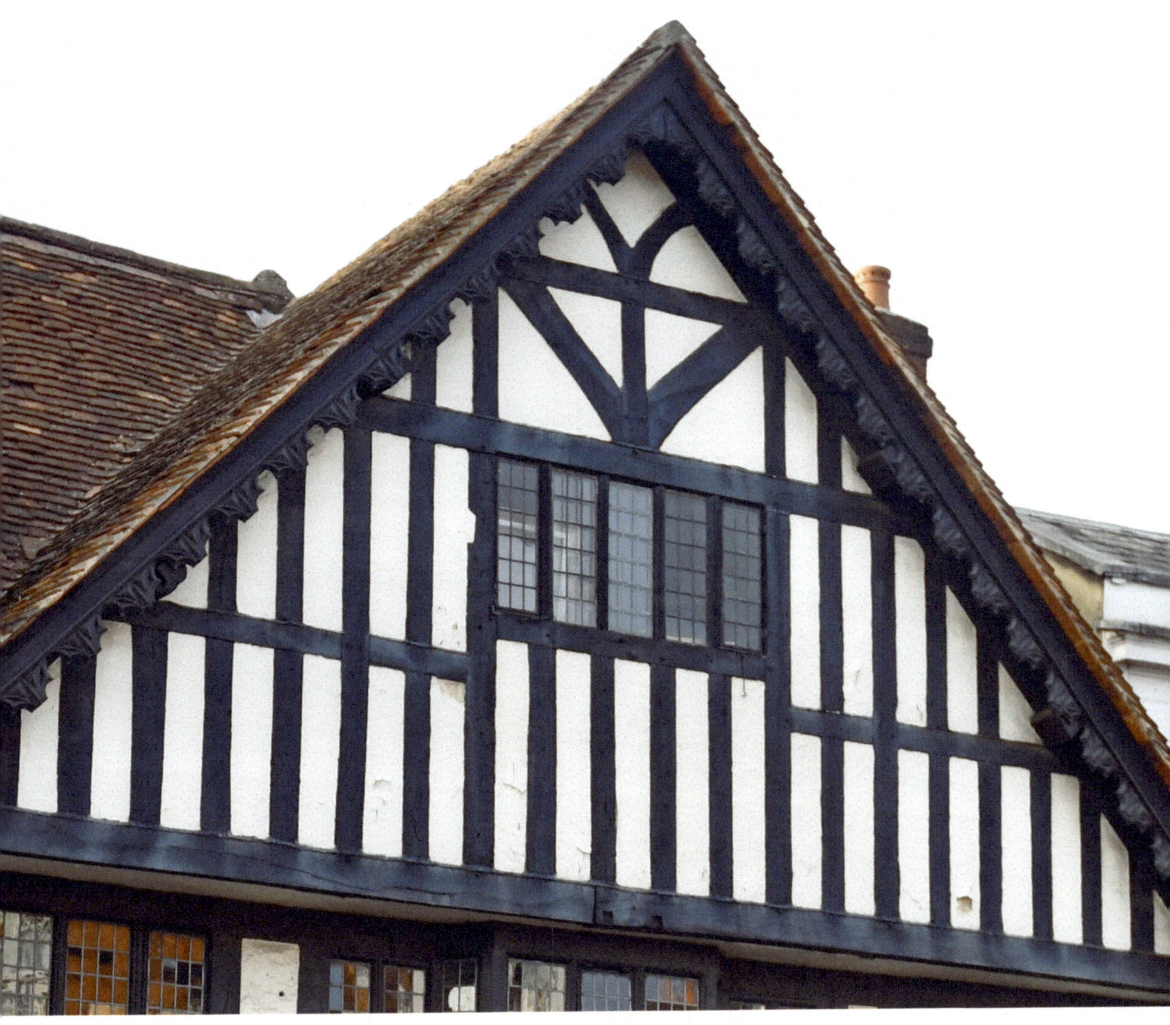

The gable on the house and shop on The Borough has a tiled roof, timber framing and decorated bargeboards.

9. Andrew Windsor's Almshouses, Castle Street, 1619

In 1619 a block of four uniform gabled almshouses were laid out on Castle Street by Andrew Windsor to accommodate eight poor people. The wide brick-built building has four gables and a brick roof. Each of the gabled units houses two residential units, with an independent doorway to the individual units at either end. Each of the doors is accessed with a short flight of steps and has a hood moulding at the top. The gable units have a pair of sash casement windows at ground-floor level and a single double-sash window at the attic level. During the nineteenth century each of the gables was given a decorated bargeboard, each with a central slim finial on the apex. The block also has a central brick stepped

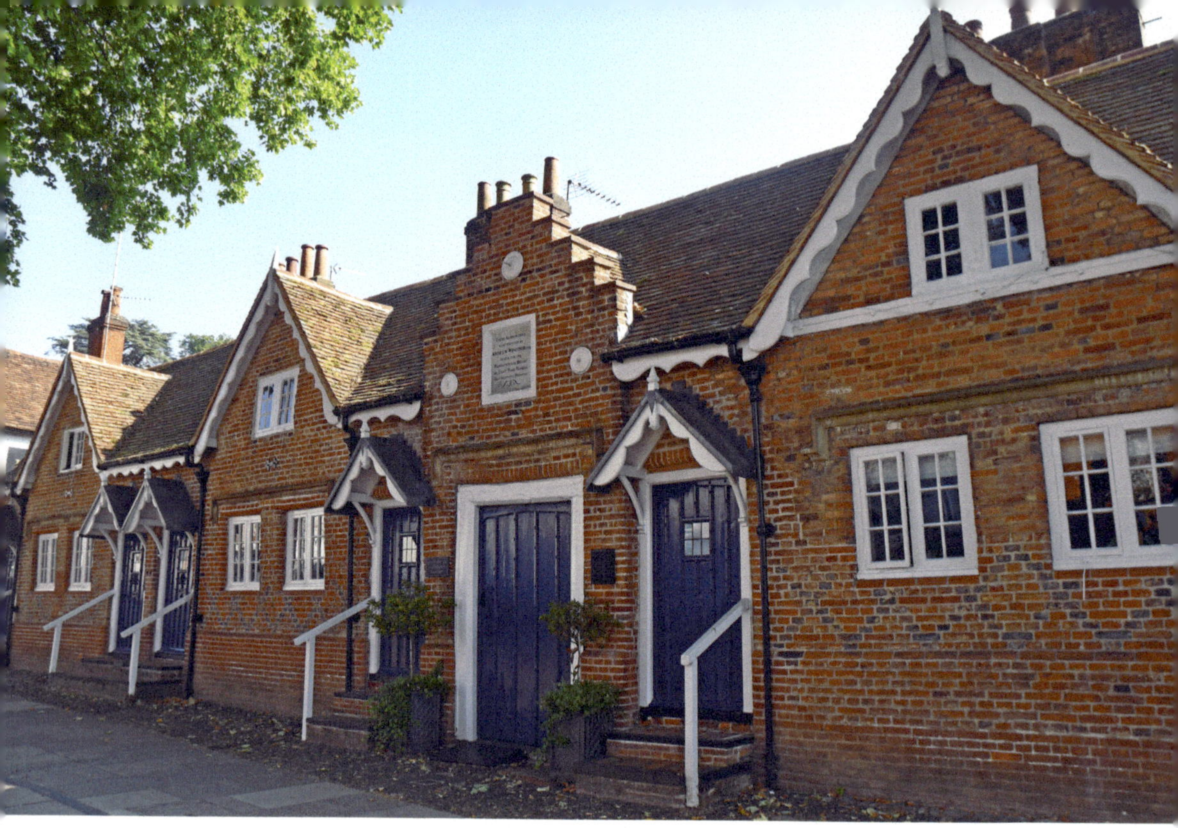

Above: The terrace of almshouses erected on Castle Street by Andrew Windsor in 1619.

Below: Each of the residential units of the Andrew Windsor almshouse has three casement windows, two side doors and decorated bargeboards.

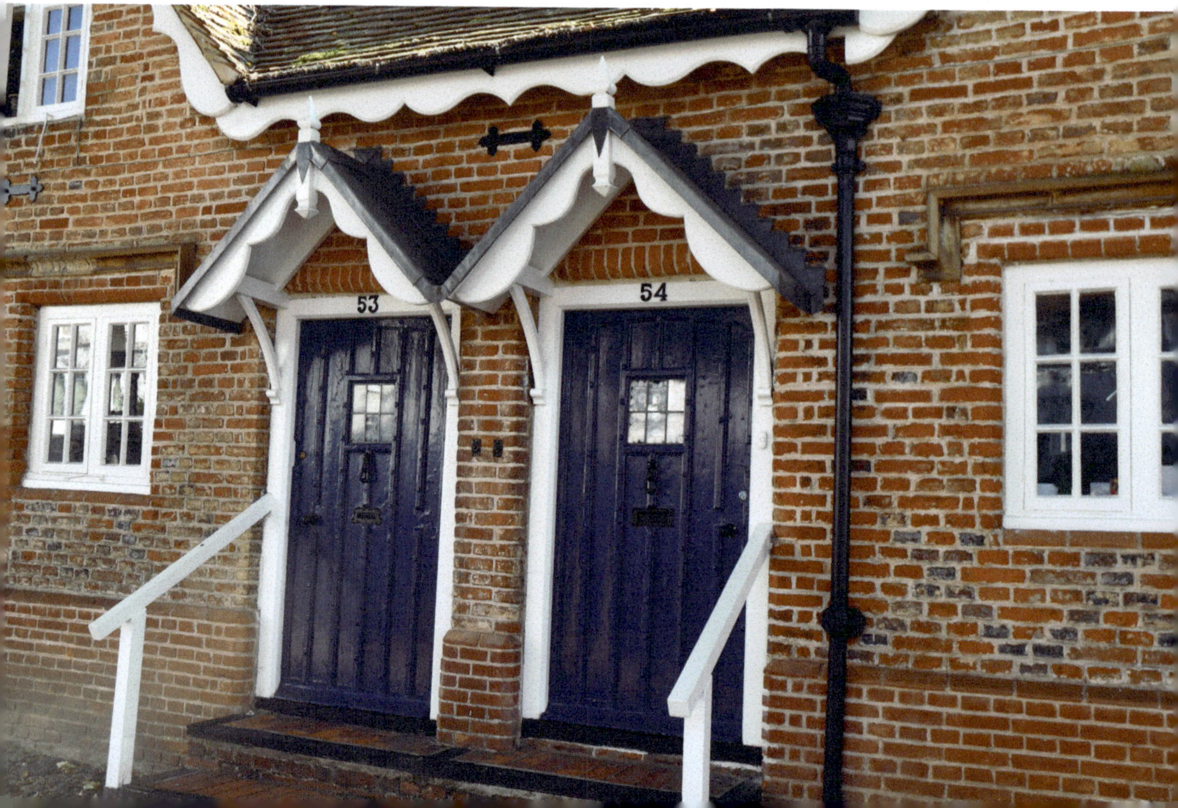

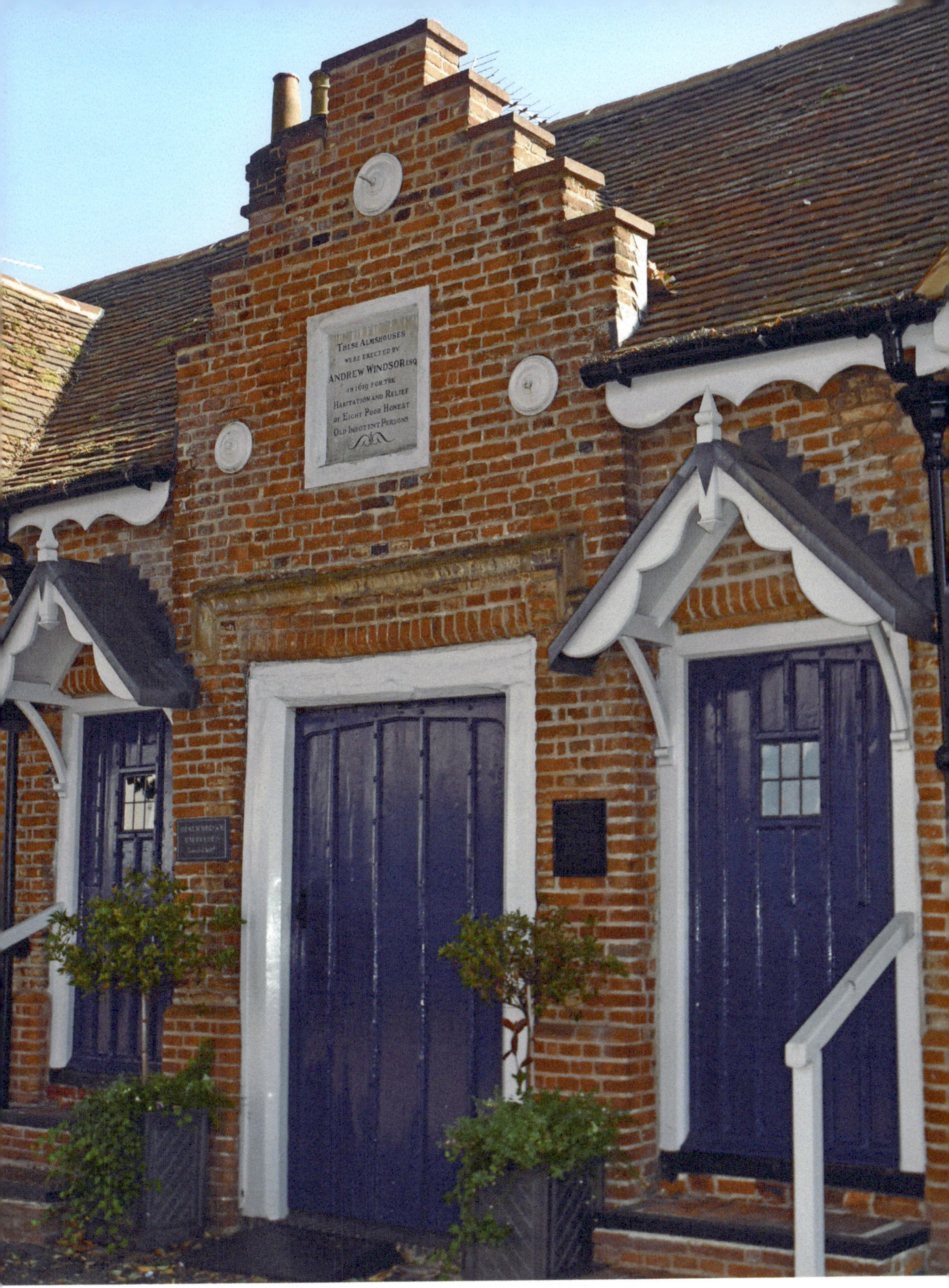

The central crow-stepped gable has a wide doorway to the rear and a date stone of 1690 marking the erection of almshouses by Andrew Windsor.

gable with a wide doorway and date stone inscribed with '1619' and the name 'Andrew Windsor'. An attractive streetscape feature is the three mature plain trees that front the building on the footpath.

10. Symmetrical Two-storey House, Downing Street, 1717

During the early part of the eighteenth century, brick-built Georgian houses began to make an appearance in Farnham. The two-storey detached house on Downing Street, formally known as Longbridge House, dates from 1717 and represents one of the earliest Georgian houses laid out in the town. This has Georgian windows spaced across the brick front and a slightly projecting central entrance bay, which features the panelled entrance door, wooden door surrounds, elaborate brick surrounds, and a moulded hood. The doorway is approached by

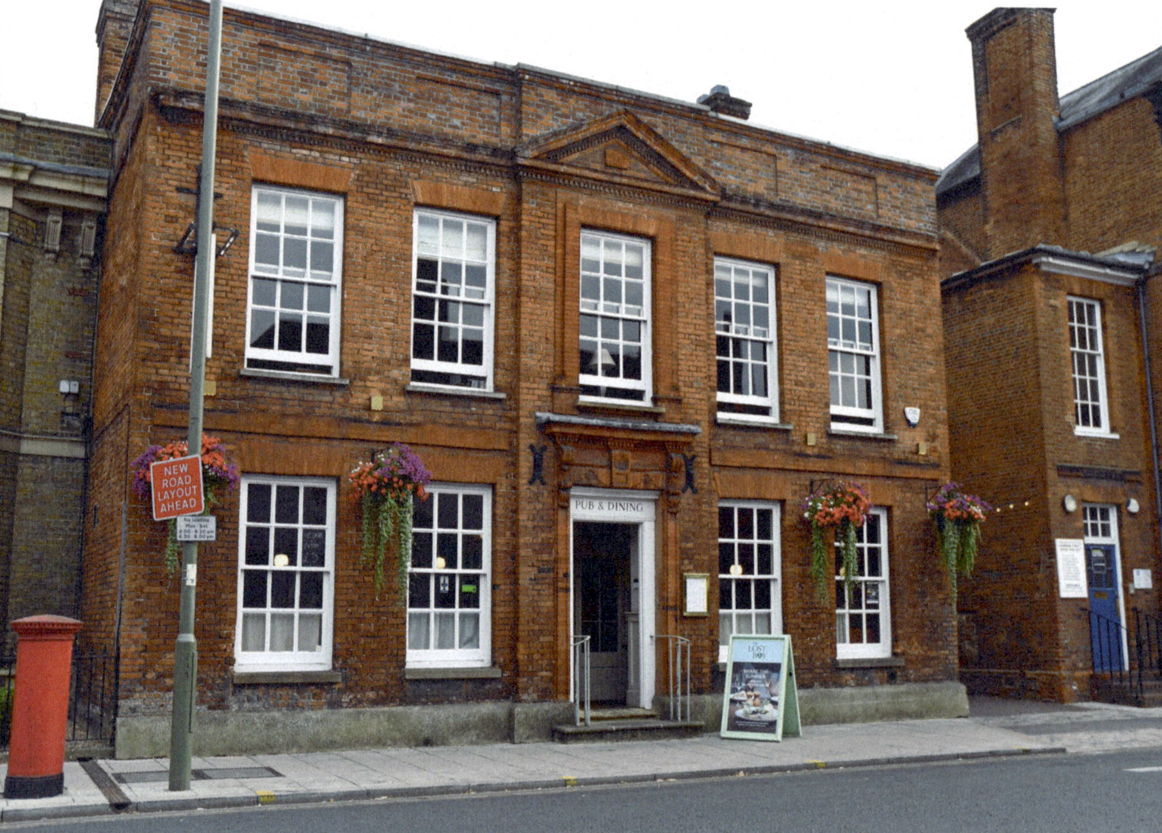

The two-storey Georgian house on Downing Street has a symmetrical brick front, a pattern of standard Georgian windows and a projecting central entrance bay. The central bay of the symmetrical house features a panel door, brick surrounds, a projecting head and a brick roof-level pediment with a 1717 date stone.

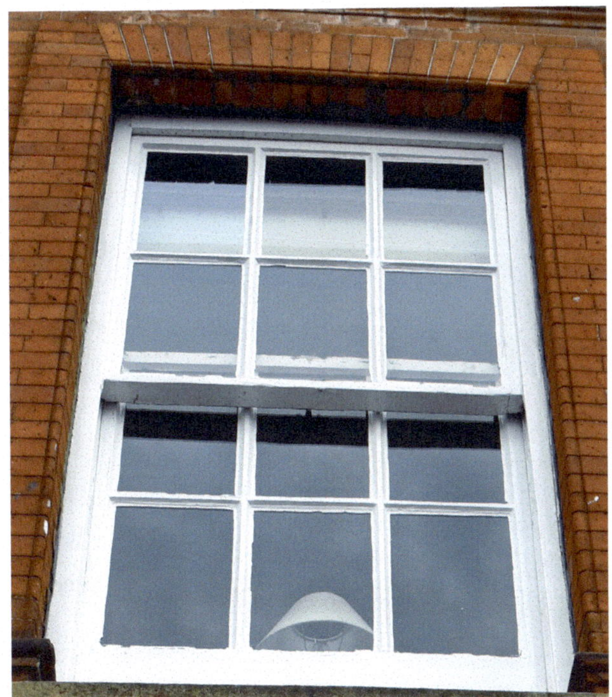

Each of the standard Georgian up and down sliding sashes of the symmetrical house on Downing Street has two sashes, six glazing panes and brick surround.

three steps and a curved metal and metal handrail. The crown of the bay has a triangular pediment at roof level with the date stone, inscribed '1717'. One of the most characteristic features of the house – and in the case of most Georgian houses – is the standard vertically proportioned timber Georgian window. This essentially consists of a pair of up-and-down sliding sashes, each with six small glazing panes. The Downing Street house has four windows on ground level and five on the first floor, all with rubbed brick surrounds. These are spaced evenly across the street elevation, separated by a brick-moulded stringcourse and broken by the central projecting bay and a brick roof parapet overhead with recessed panels. The building formally acted as a convent, although today it operates as a restaurant and pub.

11. Willmer House, West Street, 1718

Willmer House on West Street was built in 1718 by John Thorpe, a Farnham merchant, and now houses the Museum of Farnham, established in 1961. The red-brick detached three-storey building has Georgian windows on each floor level, a central entrance bay, regular brick quoins at either end, a brick moulded roof cornice and brick panelled parapet and can represent a model for many of the larger Georgian houses in Farnham. The first-floor windows have cambered heads and moulded brick surrounds. The ground- and top-floor

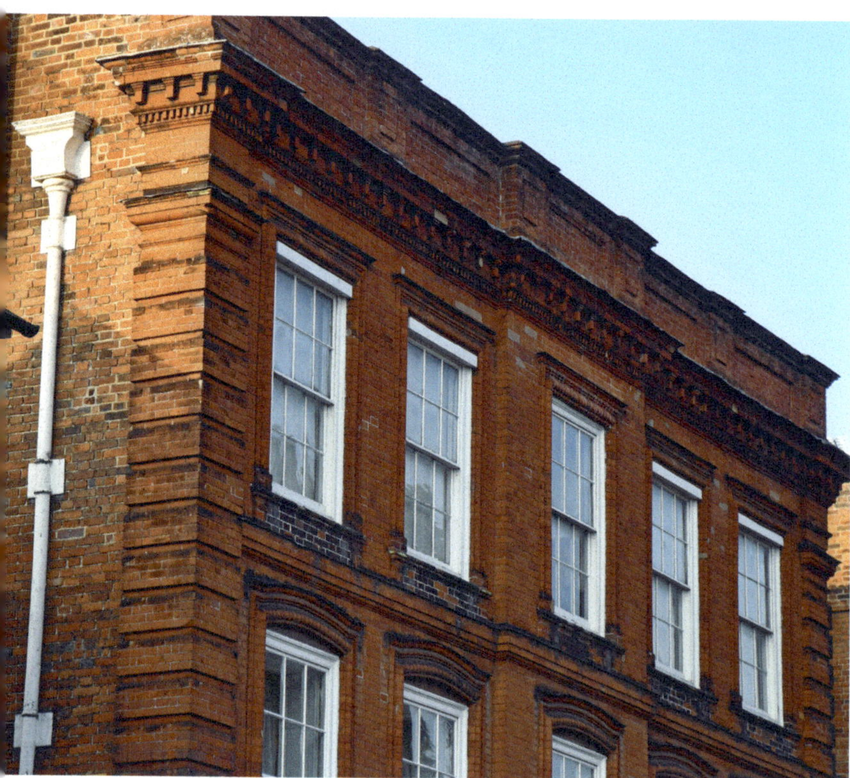

Left: The three-storey, brick Willmer House on West Street features a projecting central bay and moulded and panelled roof cornice.

Below: Willmer House has Georgian windows with moulded brick surrounds spaced uniformly across the front.

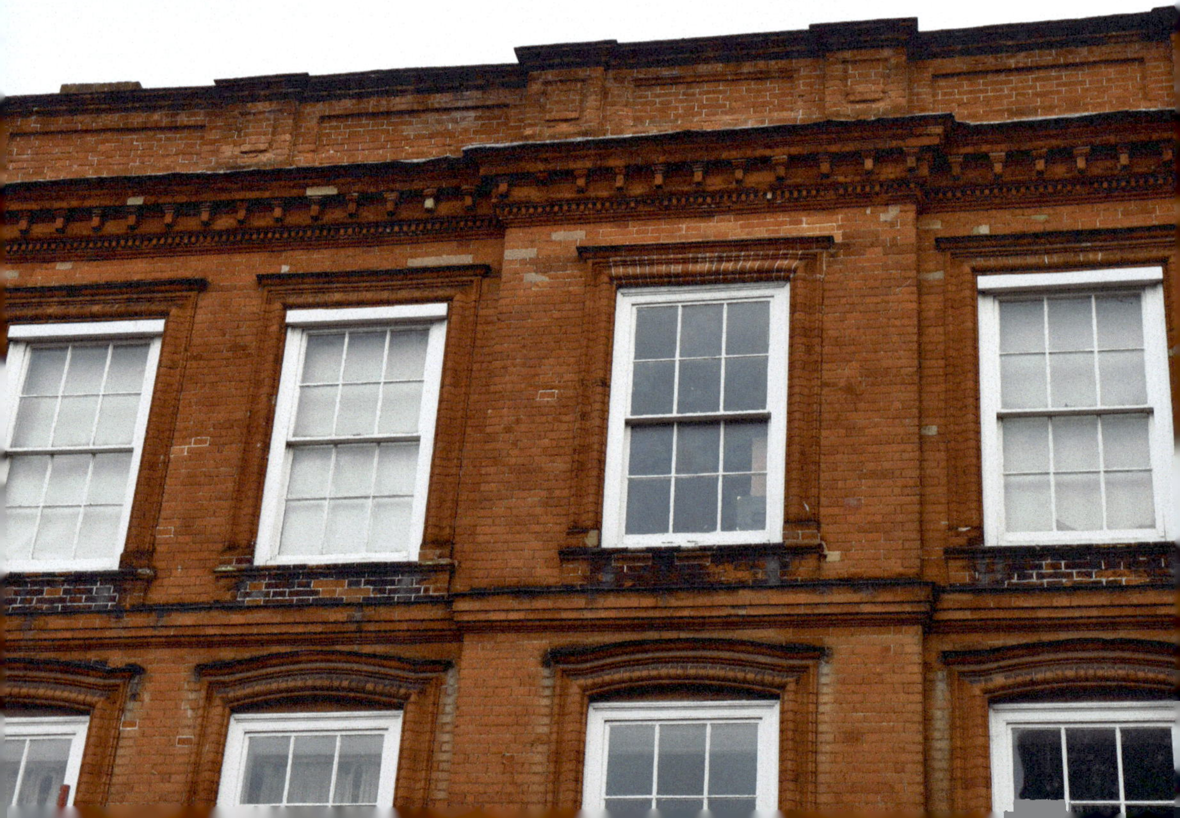

windows have brick surrounds level heads. The slightly projecting central bay has a six-panelled entrance door. This is set between panelled side columns and an overhead decorated entablature or head. The main block of the house has a kitchen extension to one side, which features a Palladian window and a door at ground level and a pair of standard Georgian windows on the first floor. The wide Palladian window is divided into three sections: a wide central sliding sash flanked on either side by a narrow sash, with the sections separated by plain uprights. The central panelled door has framed side columns, a rectangular fanlight and a projecting hood.

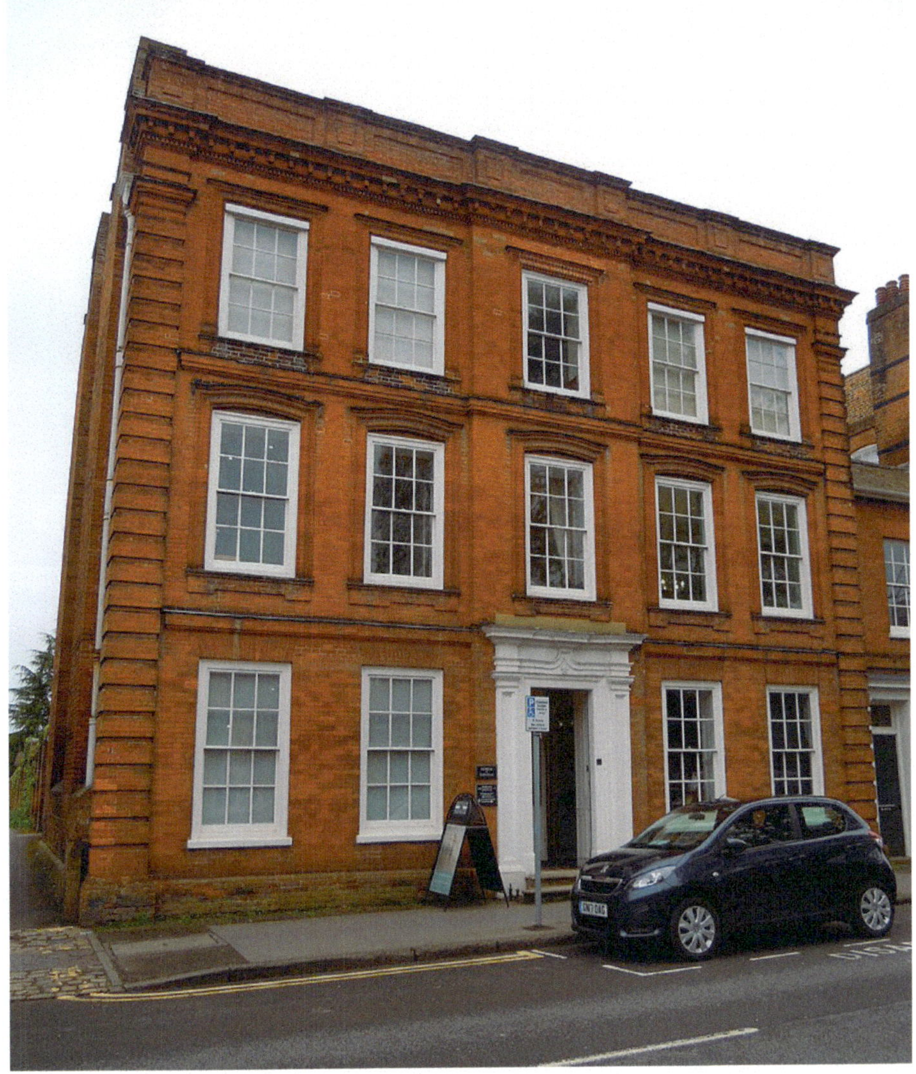

Willmer House in 2018. (Courtesy of Jack1956, CC0 1.0)

12. Town House, Castle Street, 1770

The brick house on Castle Street dates from around 1770 and was laid out in the form of a standard town house – that is with a slim front and the doorway to one side. The house forms part of a terraced streetscape, designed by George West the Elder. The house has a brick parapet, a hipped tiled roof, a single Georgian window on the ground level, a doorway to one side, and two Georgian windows on the upper-floor level. At ground level the elaborate doorcase to the side of the house is significant. Here the panelled door and overhead fanlight is set between mounded side columns that extend in a semicircular arch around the fanlight. Overhead, the open base triangular pediment is supported on projecting brackets that rest on the heads of the side columns. The doorway to the house is accessed by moulded stone steps and metal handrails. Beside the doorcase the ground-floor window is wider than the normal Georgian examples, with sixteen glazing panes rather than the more normal twelve, while the windows on the upper level have the more common arrangement of six panes per sliding sash. An unusual ground-level feature is the

Two-storey brick town house with Georgian windows and attached coach arch to one side, Castle Street.

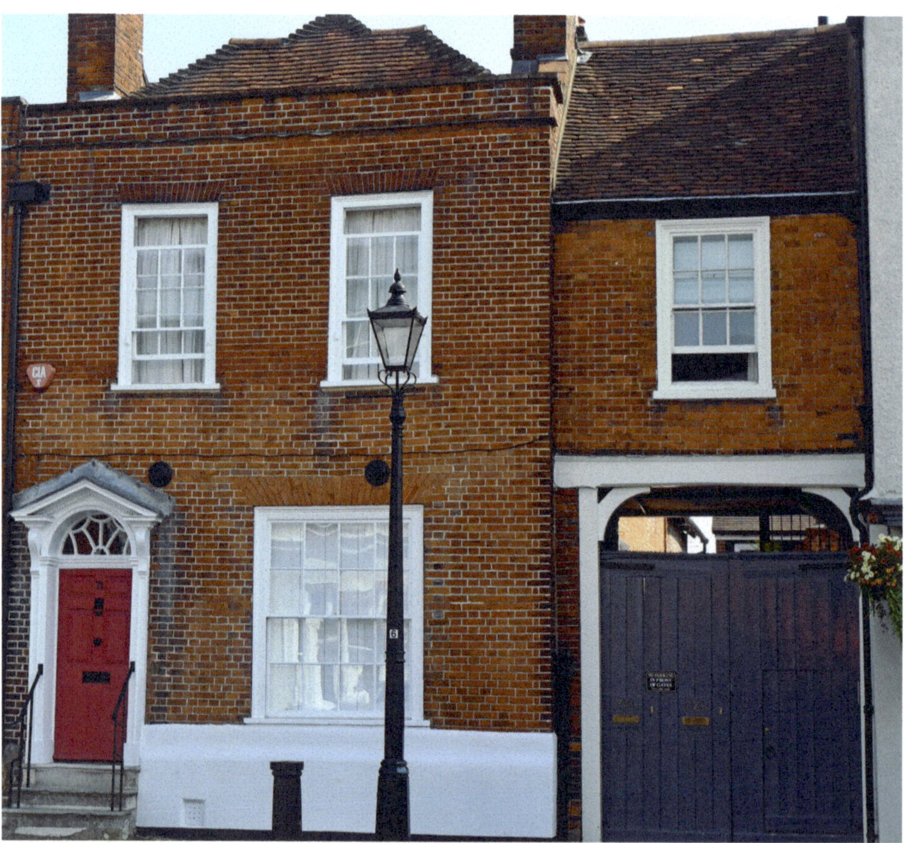

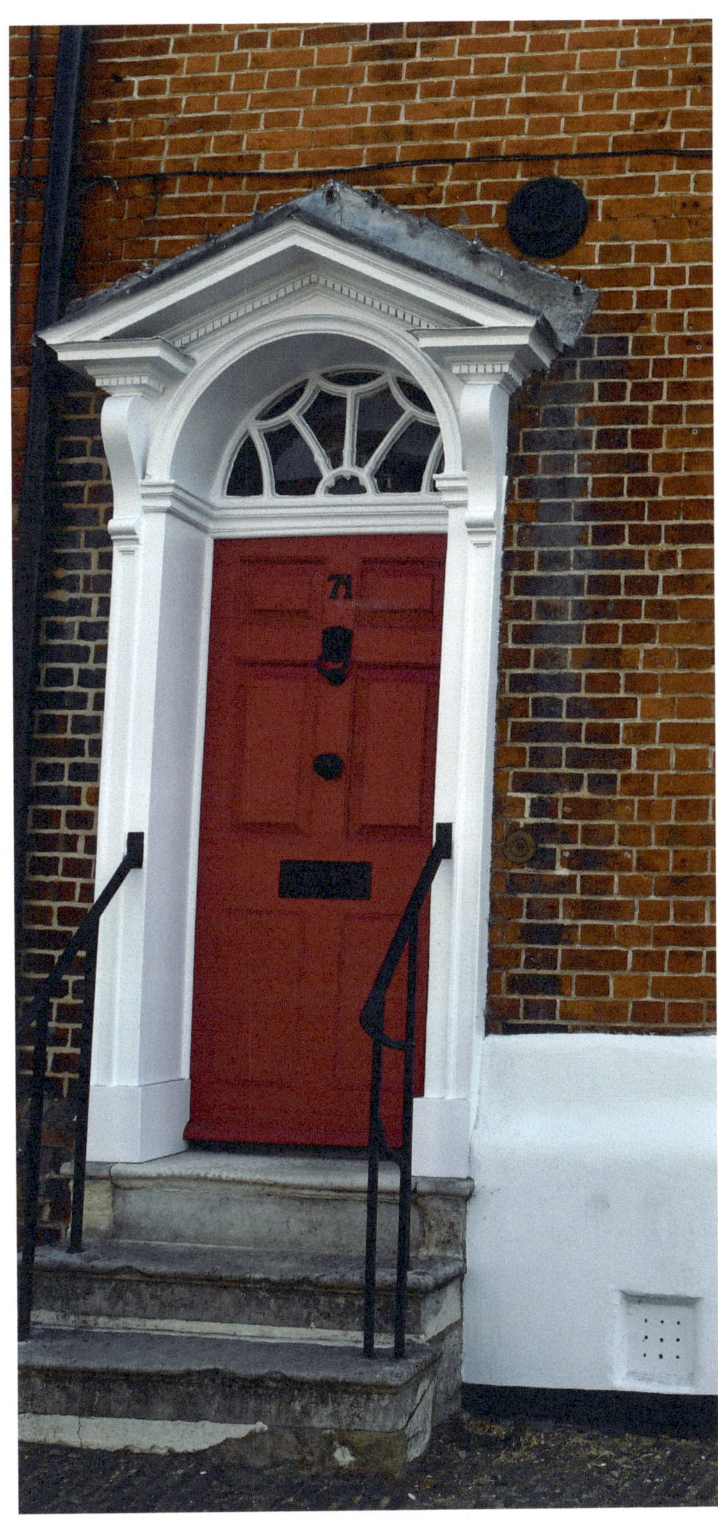

The elaborate
arched doorcase,
the town house
on Castle Street.

rendered plinth that extends downwards from the ground-level windowsill to the footpath level. At some time a brick side extension was added to the house. This has wide coach arch with a wooden sheeted door, a wooden crossbeam with curved support brackets, a single Georgian window on the first-floor level and tiled pitched roof – lower and unconnected with the hipped roof of the main house.

13. Two-storey Symmetrical House, Castle Street, 1775

The double-storey brick symmetrical house on Castle Street dates from around 1775, and forms part of an extended streetscape of two-storey houses. The ground level has a central doorcase flanked by a pair of standard Georgian sliding sashes with moulded surrounds and a lower single basement window to one side. The six-panelled door and floral-style decorated semicircular fanlight are set into a doorcase with side frames, scrolled brackets, a keystone, and an open base triangular pediment. The house is accessed by stone steps with a plain curved metal handrail on either side set into the dark brick plinth. The five first-floor Georgian windows are similar to those on the ground level and are spaced

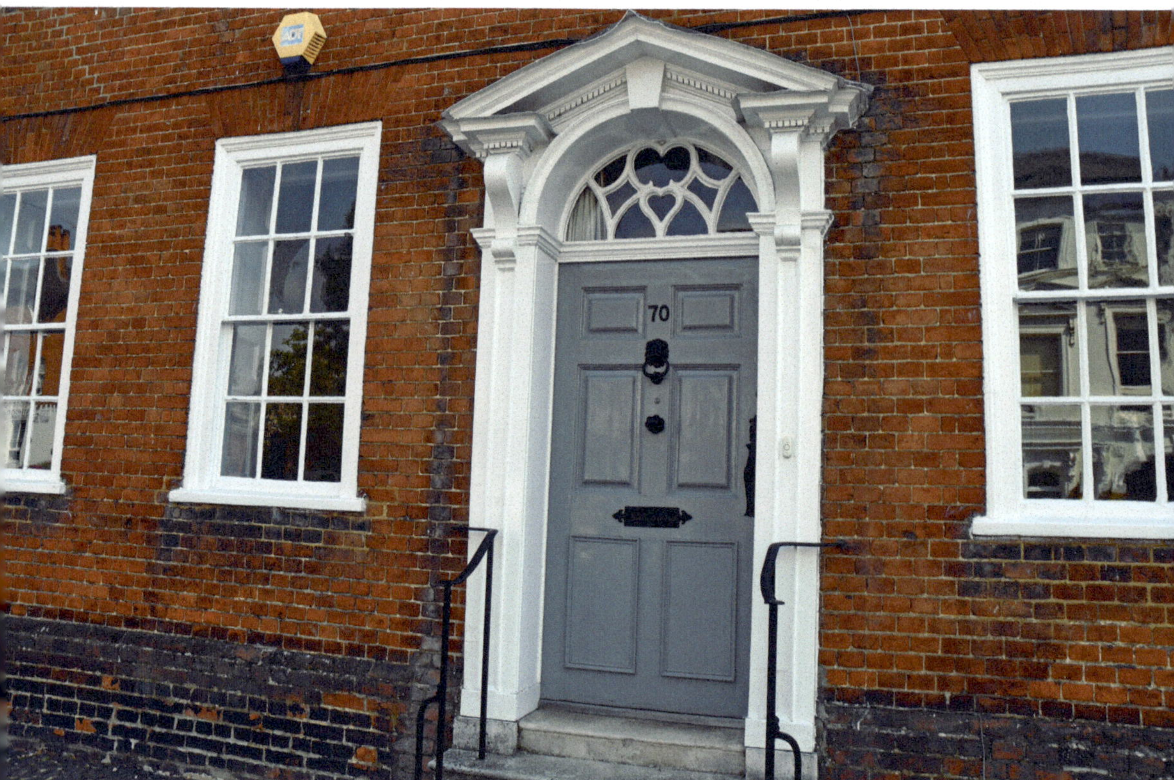

The arched and pediment central doorcase of the double-storey house on Castle Street.

equally across the front. Above this, the hipped tiled roof is partially visible behind the slightly projecting brick parapet with a stringcourse and stone coping.

14. Three-storey Symmetrical House, Downing Street, Eighteenth Century

The large asymmetrical brick three-storey house with side wings on Downing Street dates from around 1737 and has two stringcourses marking the three floor levels of the block. The central ground-floor entrance is marked with a forward-projecting single-storey porch flanked on either side by a pair of standard Georgian sliding sash windows. The porch has moulded steps and a pair of circular fluted columns and a flat roof with moulded eaves. This is flanked on either side by two Georgian windows with fifteen panes. The five first-floor windows are similar and evenly spaced across the elevation, although the five similarly spaced shorter windows on the second floor have twelve panes. The main block has two-storey stepped back side wings with flat roofs at either end. These have tall Georgian window on each floor, except for the left wing which has a panelled and glazed door at ground level. The hipped roof has a projecting cornice and lead drainpipe at each corner.

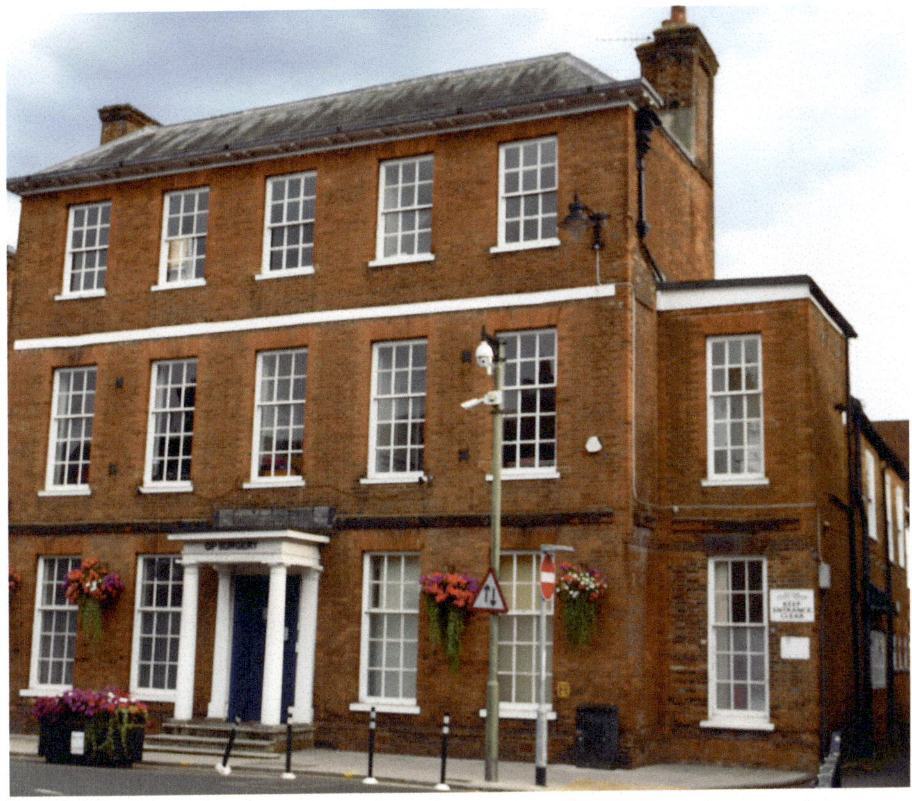

The large, asymmetrical, brick, three-storey house with side wings faces onto Downing Street.

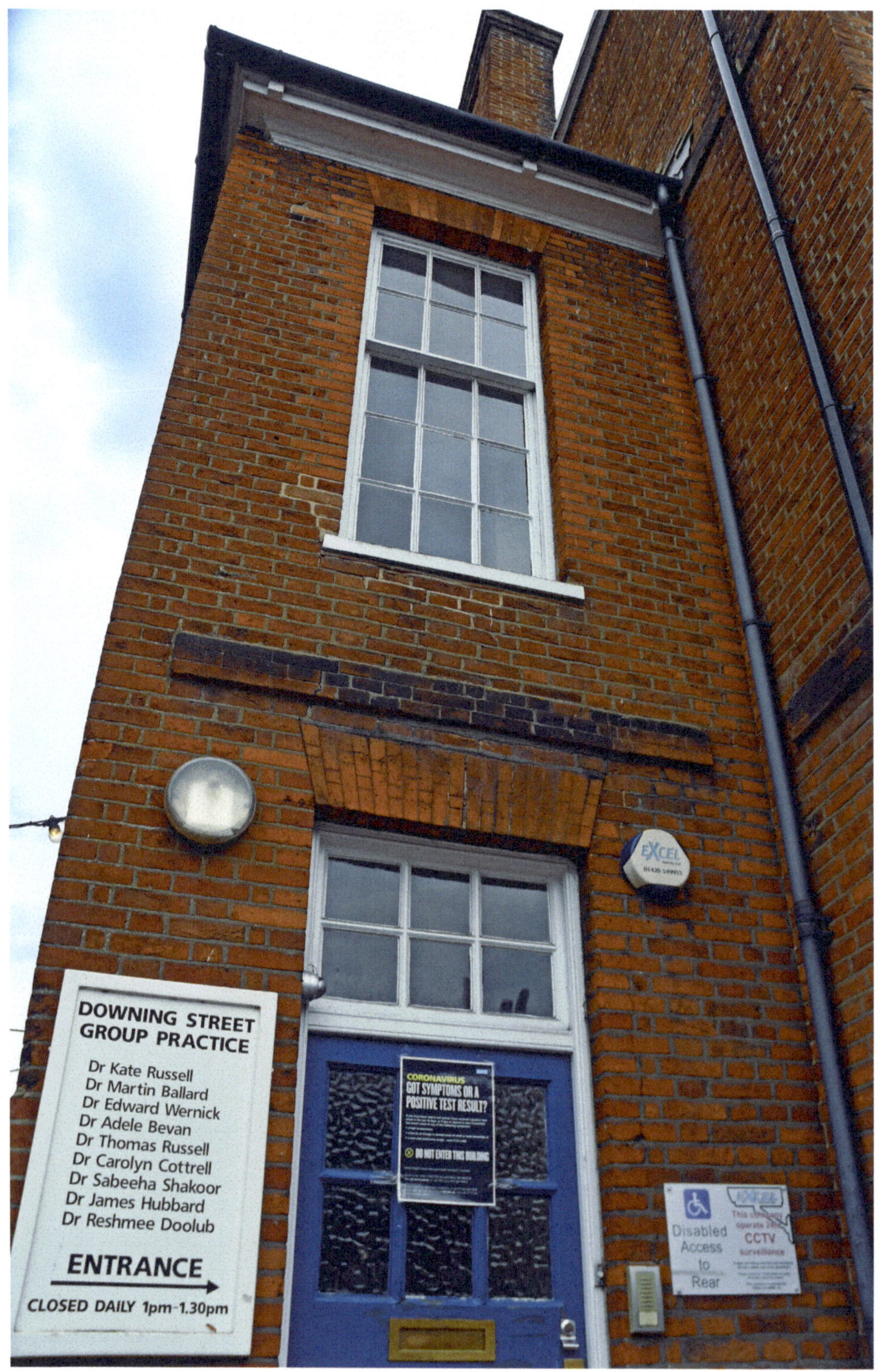

The double-storey side wing of the Downing Street house has a Georgian window, panelled door and a rectangular fanlight.

15. Freemasons' Hall, Castle Street, Eighteenth Century

The large independent brick gable-faced Freemasons' Hall faces onto Castle Street and dates from the eighteenth century. Once a schoolhouse, the building now functions as the Freemasons' Hall. This has a double-storey restrained street elevation divided into three bays . The central projecting bay has three Georgian windows on each floor level. The upper-floor Georgian windows have rounded heads with a brick relieving arch over the central opening, above which the gable has a brick eaves. The single Georgian windows of the side bays are similarly arranged with a doorcase near the corner of the left-hand bay. This has a panelled

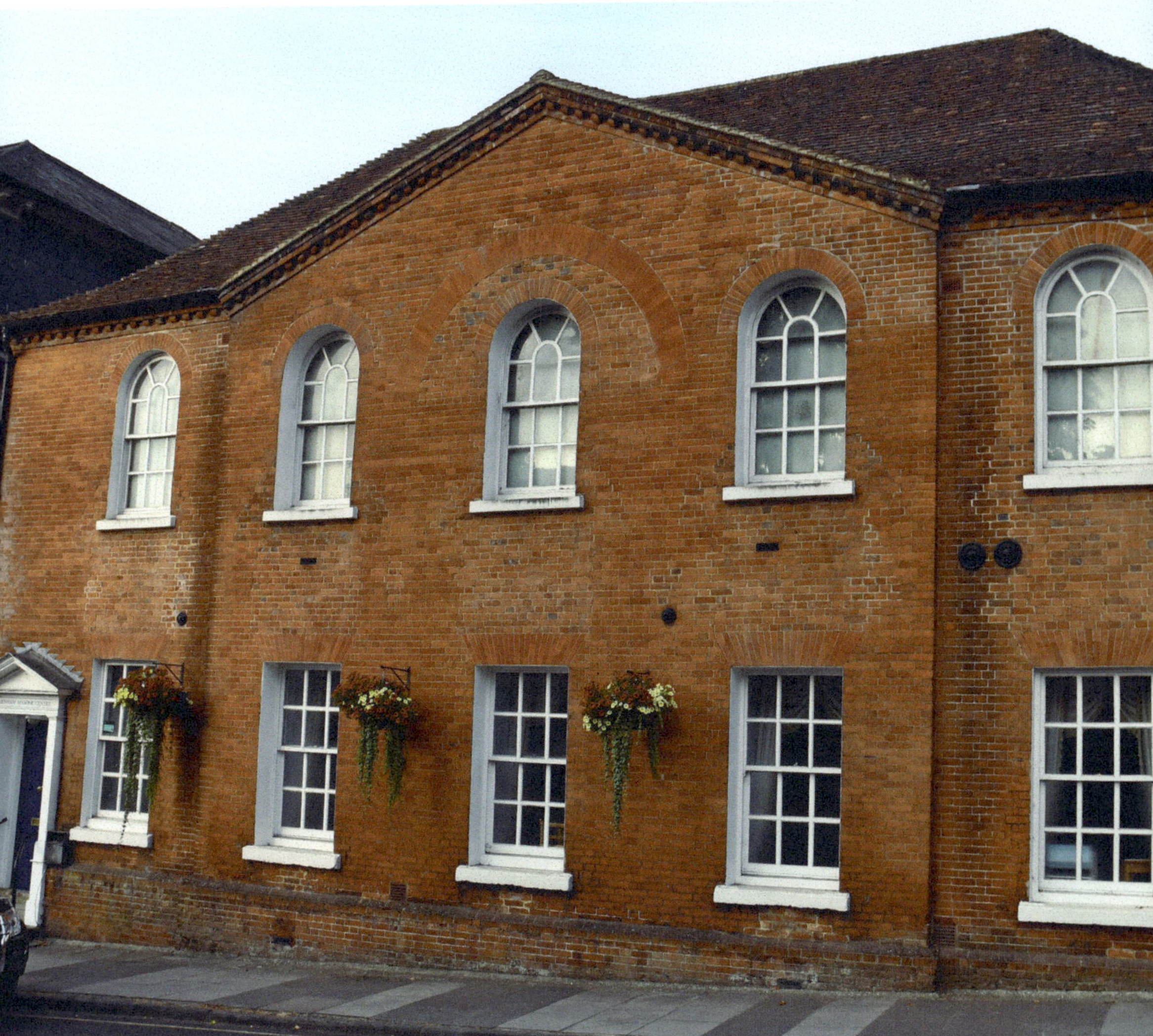

The gable front of the Masonic Hall faces onto Castle Street.

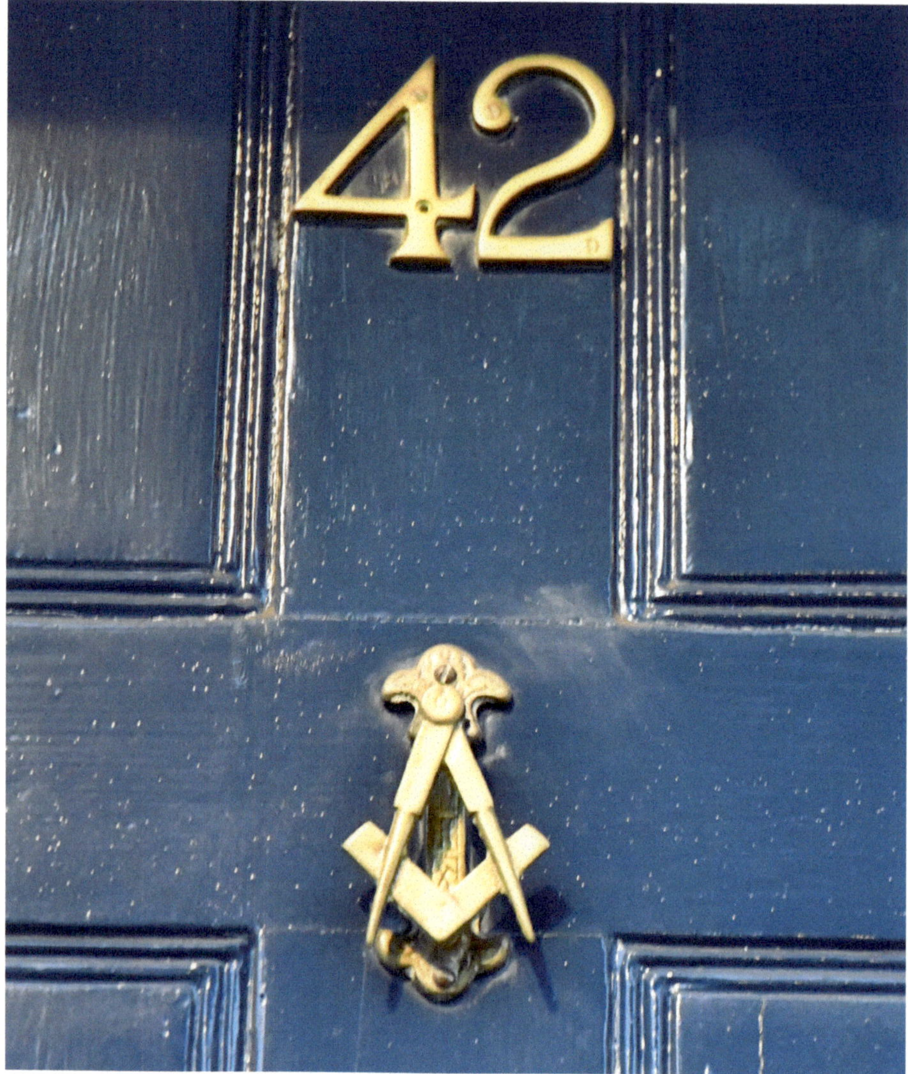

The panelled door of the Masonic Hall on Castle Street features a brass Masonic symbol and a house number.

door, flat side columns and a triangle pediment. On the north facing side elevation of the hall is a blocked-up brick arch with a cut keystone.

16. Two-storey Symmetrical House, Castle Street, Eighteenth Century

The brick symmetrical house on Castle Street, which dates from around 1720, is two storeys high with an attic positioned at one end of a stepped terrace. The ground level has a central doorway flanked on either side by a pair of

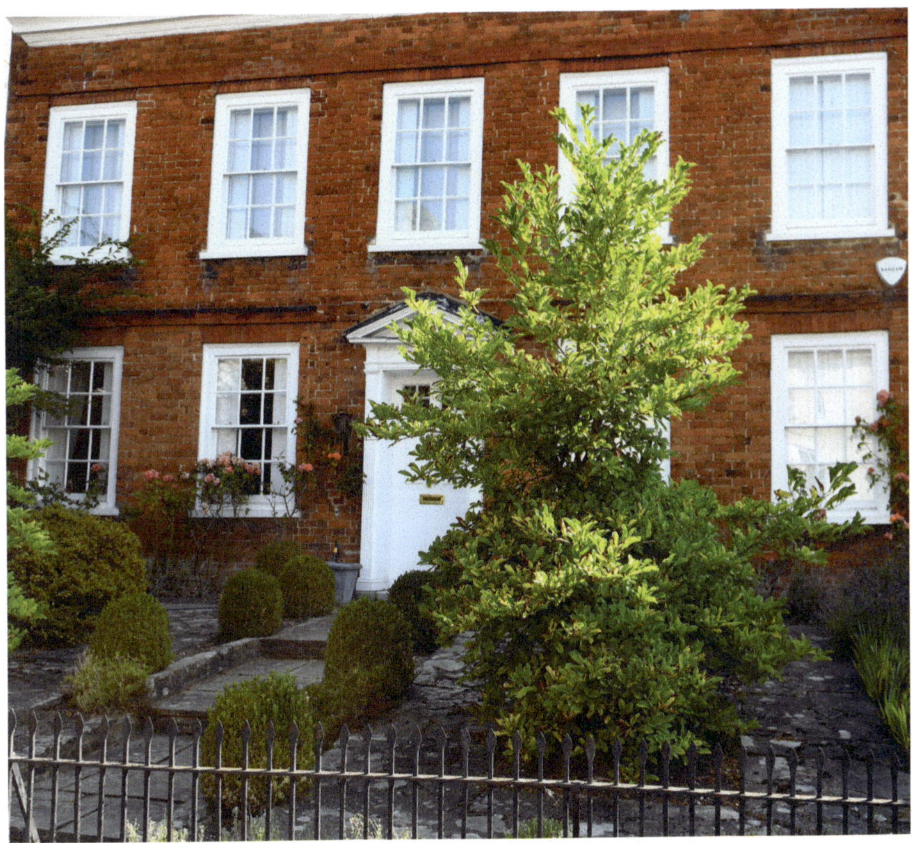

The symmetrical house on Castle Street has a landscaped front garden.

Georgian windows, beneath a projecting brick stringcourse. The windows have twelve pane sliding sashes and moulded surrounds. The central doorcase has a partially glazed panelled door with moulded side frames and a triangular pediment. The first floor has five windows, similar to those on the ground level and spaced equally across the elevation. The tiles roof has a moulded cornice and three gabled dormer windows, each with double leaded glazed sashes, wooden framing and tiled hipped roofs. In an unusual instance, the house has a landscaped front garden.

17. Two-storey House, Castle Street, Eighteenth Century

The double-storey brick house on Castle Street is one of a matching pair of semi-detached houses with dormer windows that share a massive chimney stack. A notable feature of the house is the tripartite Palladian windows on both levels. The single ground-floor window is divided into a central Georgian sliding sash with

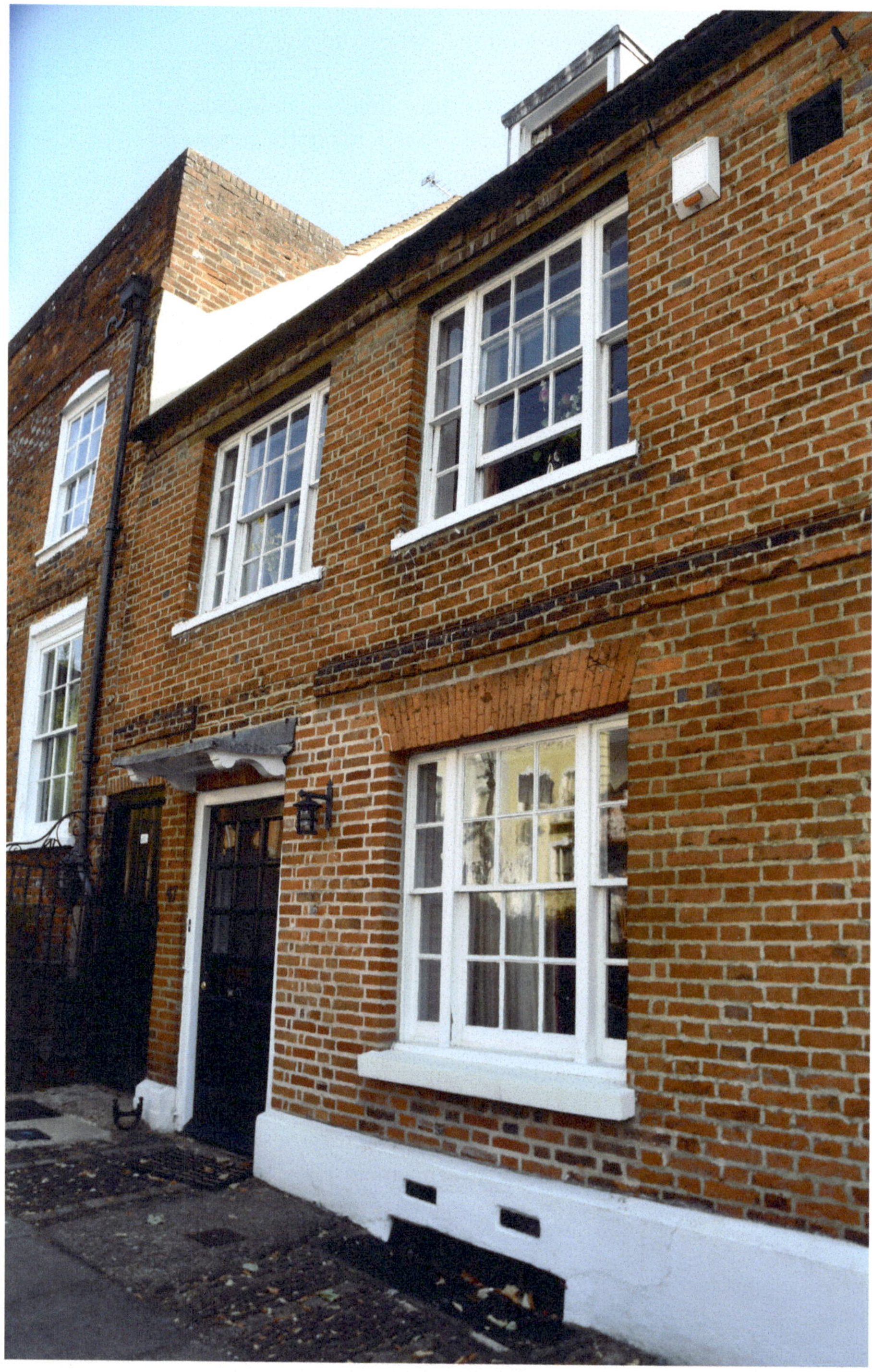

The double-storey brick house with tripartite Palladian windows on Castle Street.

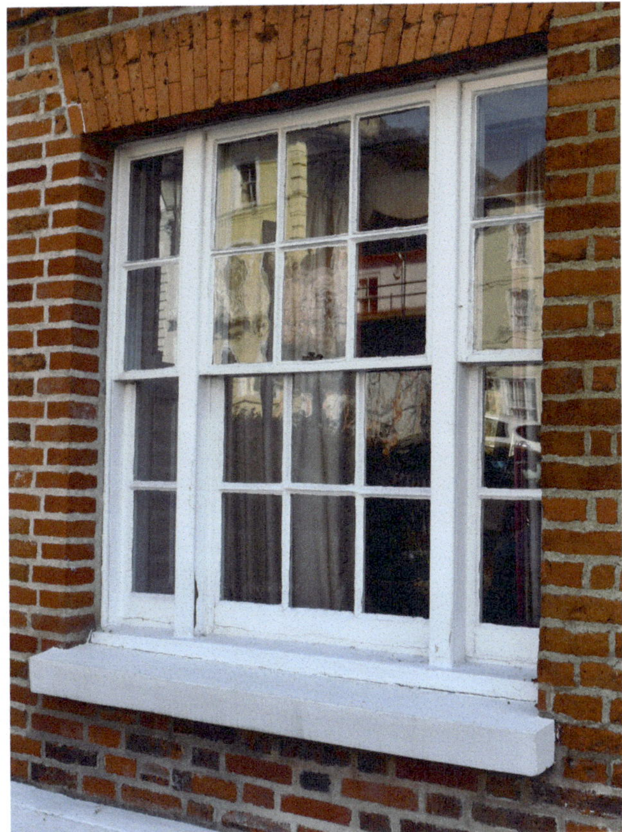

The Palladian tripartite window of the Castle Street house has a wide central sash and a pair of narrow side sashes.

small panes, flanked by two narrow sashes separated by wooden mullions; the upper floor has a pair of similar windows. The different floor levels of the house are defined by a continuous projecting brick stringcourse. The entrance doorway on the left-hand side of the front has a half-glazed door with a flat canopy. The house also has a side door beside the main entrance doorway. The tiled roof has a brick eaves and a slightly off-centre dormer window. This has a six-pane casement sash and a lead sheeted roof and sides.

18. Two-storey Symmetrical House, Castle Street, Eighteenth Century

The front elevation of the two-storey brick house with a basement on Castle Street has an unusual combination of arched window bays, a slightly projecting central bay, stringcourses above each of the window heads, and an irregularly arranged window pattern. The doorcase in the central bay has a panelled door, moulded side columns, a radial decorated semicircular fanlight, and an open base triangular pediment. The doorway has two stone steps flanked by a pair of foot scrapers – an unusual surviving feature. The ground floor has two wide windows

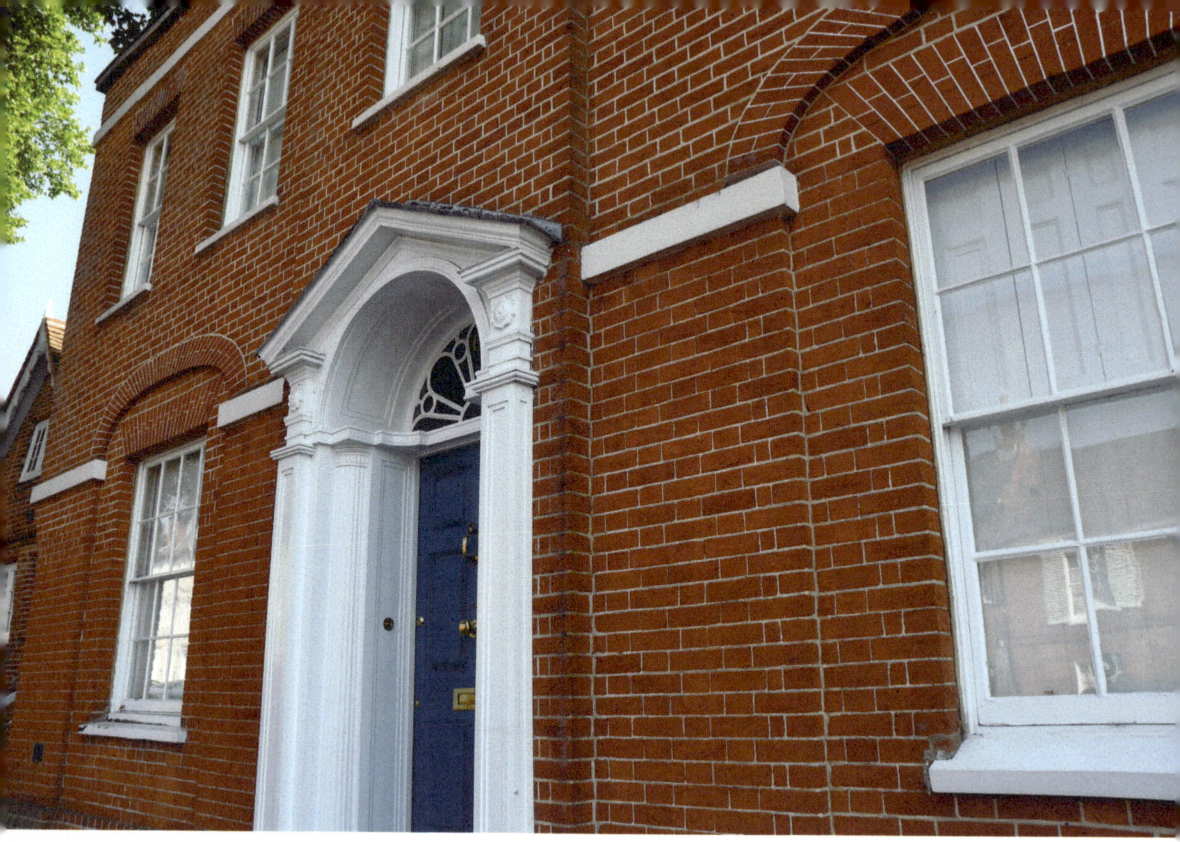

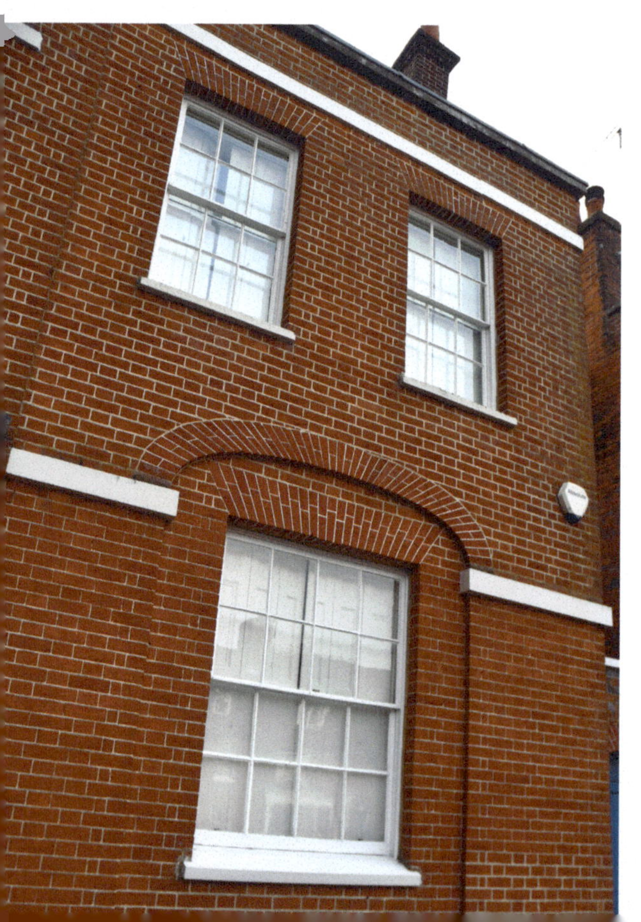

Above: The distinctive double-storey symmetrical house on Castle Street features arched, recessed window bays, a stepped central bay and pronounced stringcourses.

Left: The wide Georgian ground-level windows of the house on Castle Street are set into recessed arched openings.

with sixteen panes. These are set into wide recessed archways, partially broken by the line of the stringcourse. Overhead the five first-floor Georgian windows are spaced evenly across the elevation. The central round-headed window has a keystone and imposts. On the upper level, the tiled roof is partially screened by the brick parapet. The house has a single-storey brick-built garage attached to the adjoining house and the basement floor of the house is served by a small low-level ventilator beneath each of the ground-level windows.

19. Two-storey Symmetrical House, Castle Street, Eighteenth Century

The two-storey symmetrical brick house on Castle Street is similar in scale to the adjoining house, although in this case the central doorcase is flanked by a pair of standard Georgian window sashes at ground level and the house was given

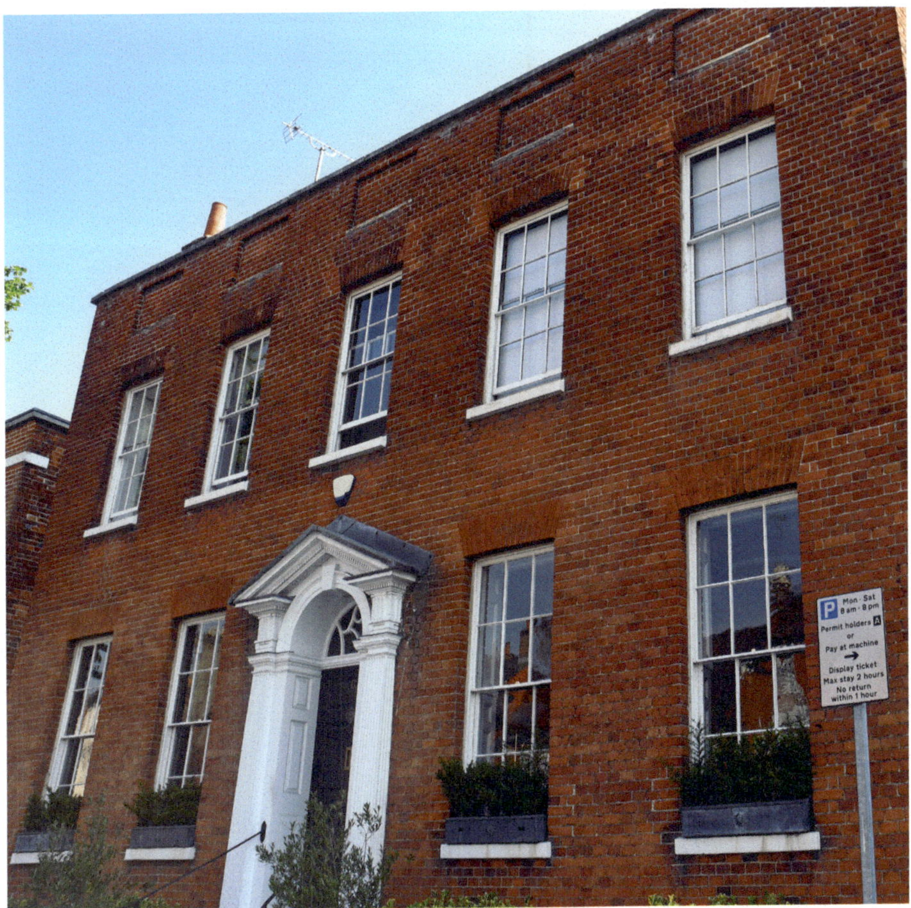

The two-storey symmetrical brick house on Castle Street has a central doorcase, Georgian sash windows and a recessed panelled brick parapet.

a tall dark brick plinth. The central doorway is accessed by six moulded stone steps with a curved metal handrail. The doorcase has a panelled door flanked by moulded and framed side columns, with the line carried around the decorated semicircular fanlight, crowned by an open base triangular pediment. Overhead, the five rectangular Georgian windows are similar and equally spaced across the front. One of the outstanding features of the house is the tall brick parapet that screens the tiled roof. This features recessed panels set in place directly over the first-floor windows.

20. Town House, Castle Street, Eighteenth Century

The two-storey end-of-terrace town house on Castle Street has Georgian windows and a side-positioned doorcase. The three upper-floor windows have cambered heads and moulded surrounds. The two ground-floor windows also have moulded

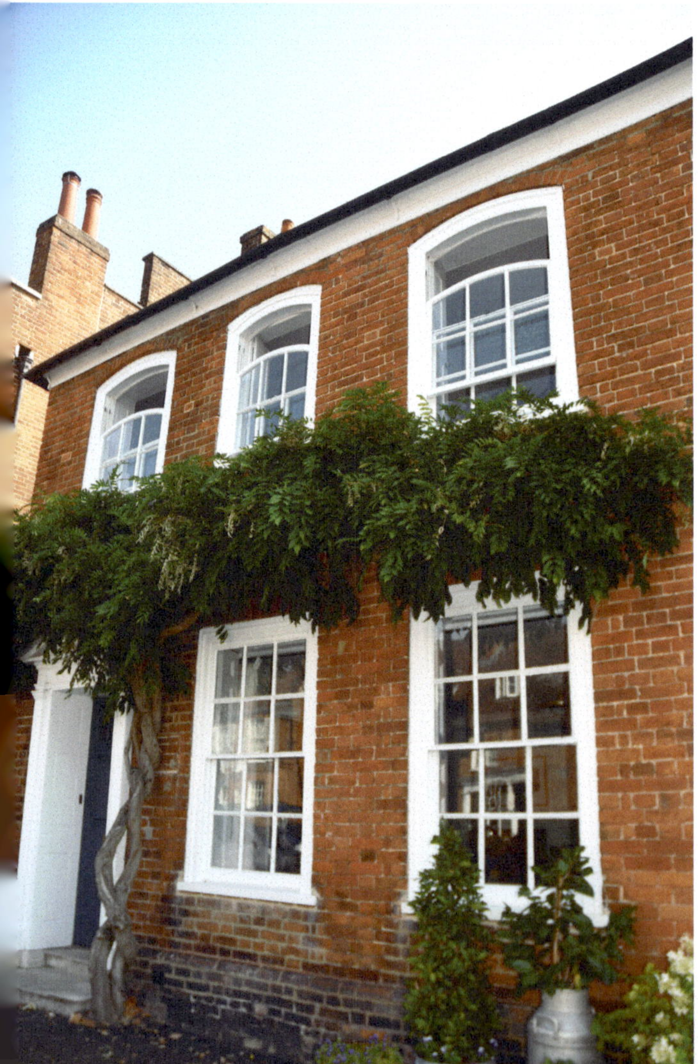

The brick, two-storey, end-of-terrace town house on Castle Street has Georgian windows and a side-positioned entrance.

surrounds, although the heads are square. The panelled door is set between moulded surrounds with an overhead wide triangular pediment. The prominent high-pitched roof is tiled and has a moulded eaves.

21. Two-storey House, Castle Street, Eighteenth Century

The narrow two-storey, symmetrical, brick, terraced house on Castle Street is part of an irregular terrace and features large window openings, recessed brick panels and a central doorway. The ground level has central panelled door with moulded side surrounds, an open base triangular pediment and a pair of wide flanking Georgian sliding windows with sixteen panes. The pair of first-floor windows is similar with a recessed blank brick panel between. Overhead the parapet also has three shallow brick panels aligned on the window and panel pattern of the first floor. The elevation also has a brick stringcourse that stretches across the front elevation and blends into the sides of the triangular pediment.

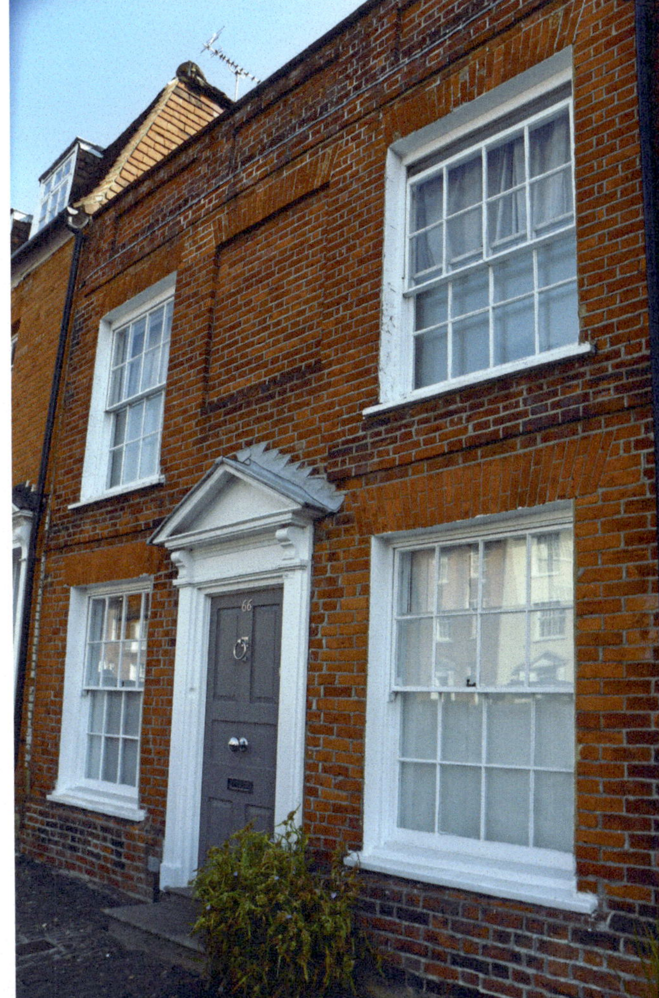

The two-storey house on Castle Street with large windows and blank brick panelling.

22. Wickham House, West Street, Eighteenth Century

The independent three-storey symmetrical Wickham House on West Street dates from the eighteenth century, with the name derived from a local family. The brick house is three storeys high with a brick parapet and moulded cornice and brick stringcourses over the window heads. The house is flanked on either side by a narrow side passage and features a central doorway and two Georgian windows on the ground floor. The six-panel door has panelled side panels, a moulded surround, a rectangular fanlight with a diagonal pattern, and a flat projecting hood with richly carved horizontal brackets. The two windows have exposed box frames with twelve panes. The first- and second-floor windows are spaced evenly across the front. These match those on the ground level, although the second-floor windows are lower with only nine panes apiece. The elevation seems to have been recently remodelled.

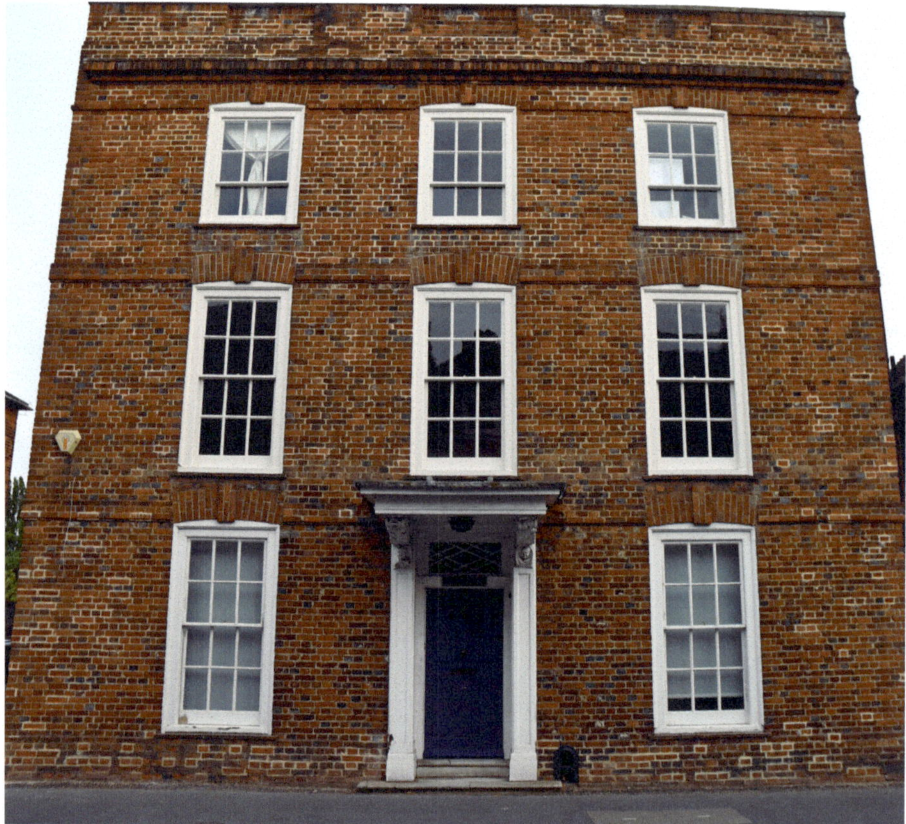

Above: Independent, symmetrical, three-storey Wickham House on West Street.

Opposite: The doorcase of Wickham House has framed surrounds and a projecting hood with brackets.

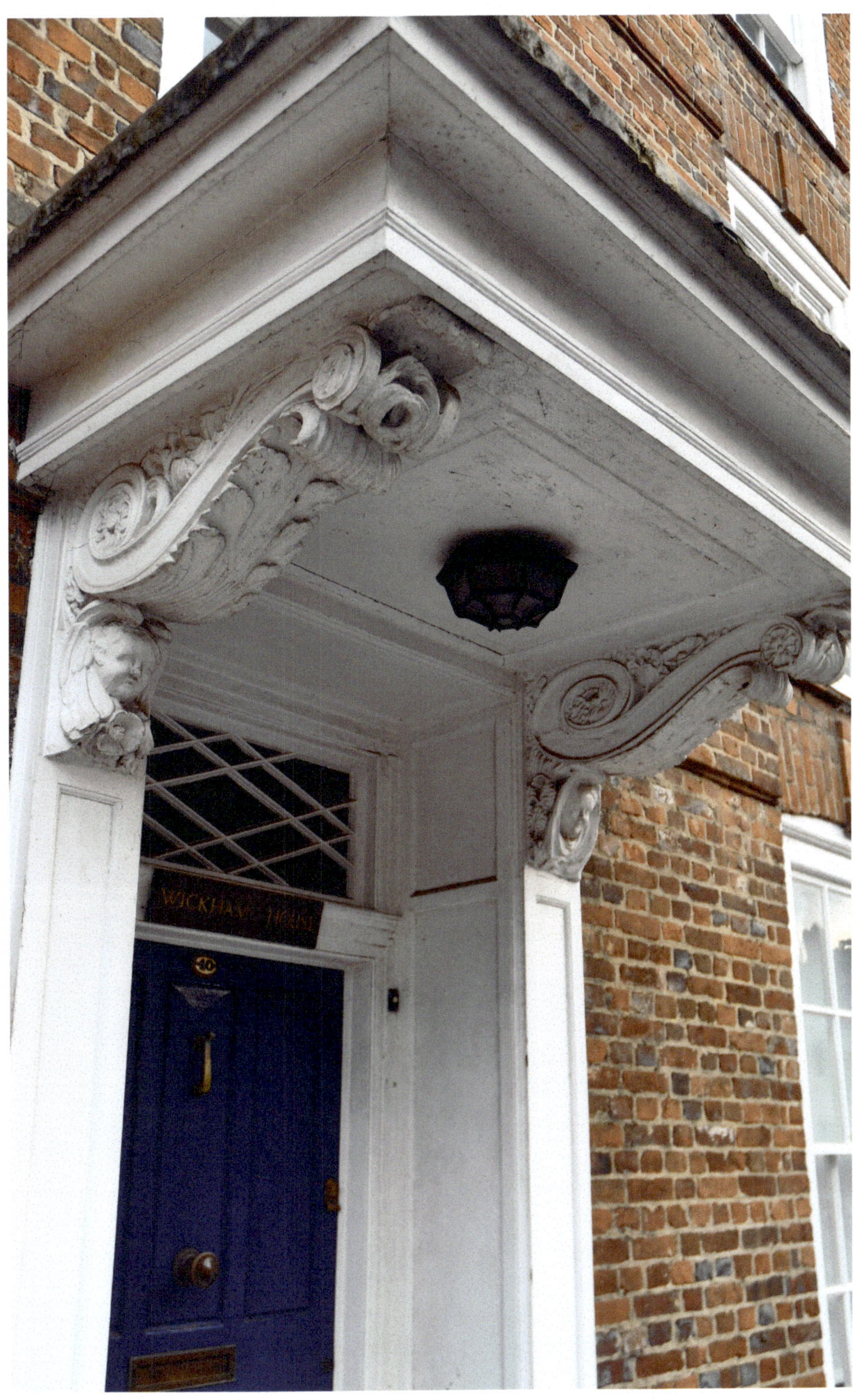
WICKHAM HOUSE
30

23. Two-storey House and Shop, Castle Street, Eighteenth Century

The house and shop on Castle Street is the end part of an extended terrace that stretches along the street. The symmetrical brick elevation has a shopfront at ground level and a pair of tripartite Georgian windows at first-floor level in addition to a single dormer window set into the slope of the tiled roof. These seem to have been added to the original house front during the nineteenth century. The shopfront extends across the full width of the building with a central framed and glazed shop door. This is set between shop display windows with large glazing panes arranged in a Georgian fashion and deep continuous fascia and roller blind that extends across the front of the building. On the first-floor level the pair of

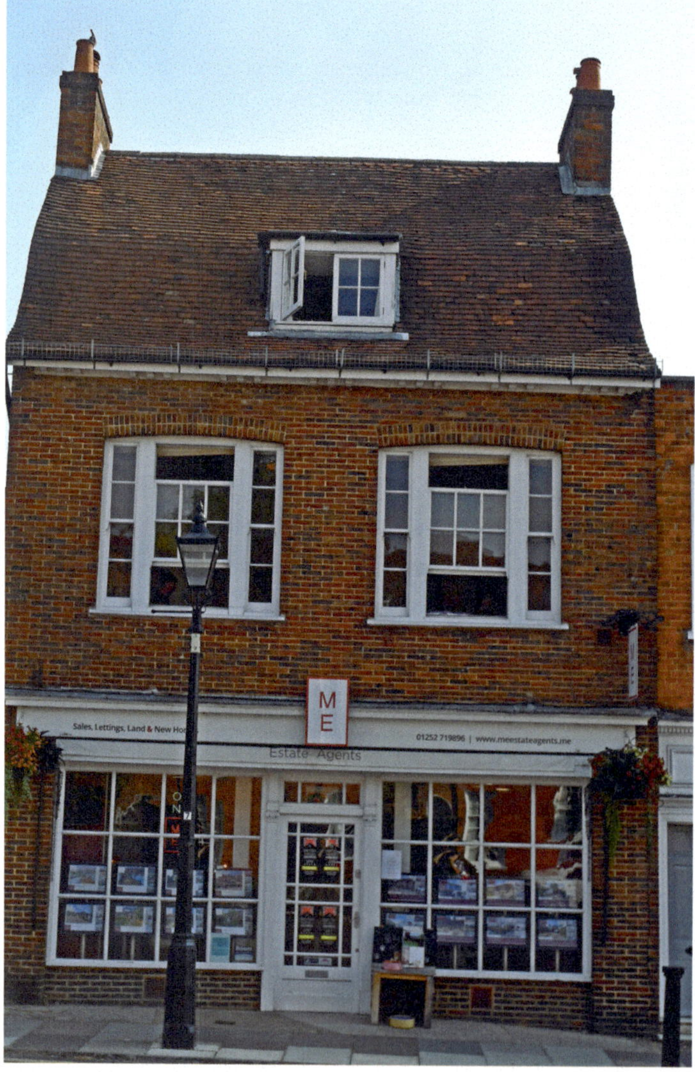

The double-storey and dormer floor of the brick house and shop on Castle Street is positioned at the end of an extended terrace.

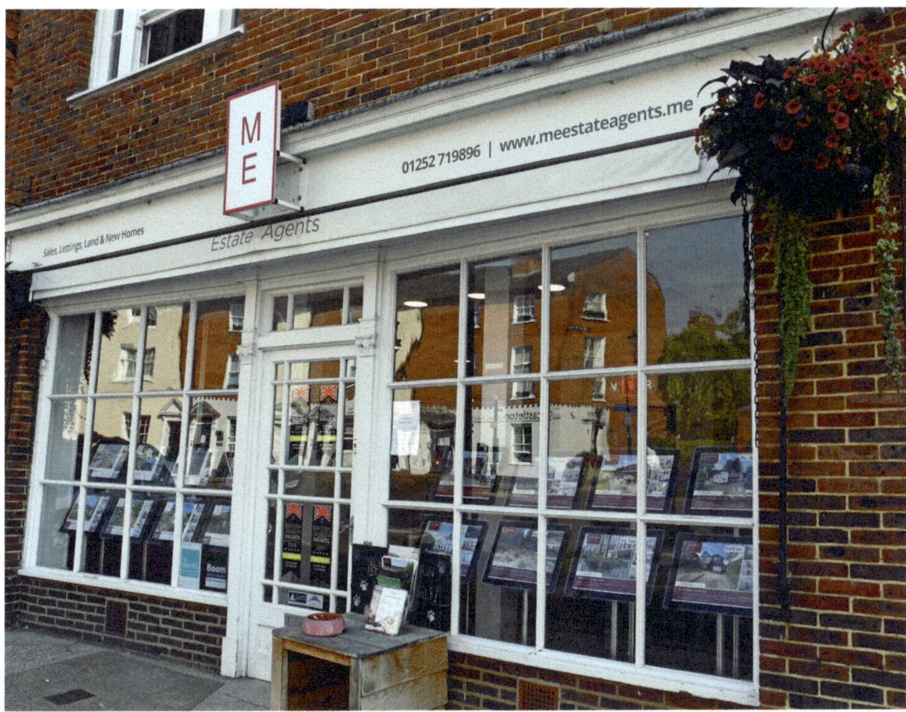

The shopfront of the house and shop on Castle Street features a central door, Georgian-style glazing and an extended fascia.

camber-headed treble-sash windows is spaced equally across the elevation. Each has a wide central sash, flanked on either side by a narrow side sash – the three separated from one another by a plain upright divider. Above the windows the tiled mansard roof has a single dormer window that is aligned centrally on the pitch. This has two side by side casement sashes, each divided into four small panes.

24. Three-storey House and Shop, Castle Street, Eighteenth Century

The three-storey house and shop building on Castle Street dates from the eighteenth century, while the ground-floor shopfront and upper-floor pebble dashing was added during the following century. The primary feature of the ground floor is the shopfront, which steps slightly outwards and has a wide display window with multiple Georgian-type panes and a glazed panel door at either end. One provides access to the interior of the unit, the other to the stairs to the upper levels, and both are emphasised by framed with side panels. Above the shopfront the moulded fascia extends across the full width of the building but steps out over the display window. Each of the two upper-level floors has a pair of Georgian

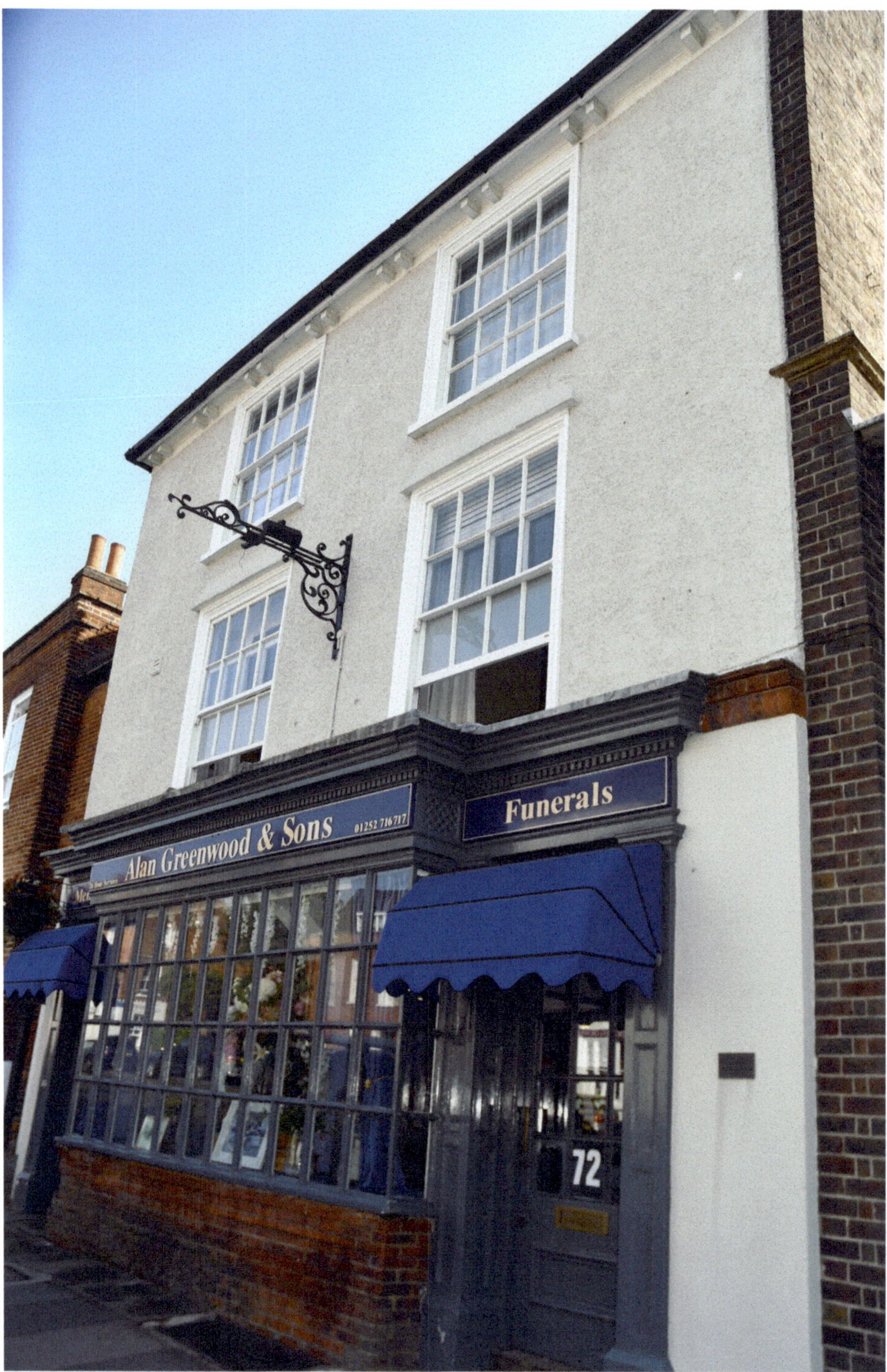

The pebble-dashed, three-storey house and shop has an elaborate Georgian-style shopfront and Georgian windows on the upper floors.

windows spaced evenly across the pebble-dashed frontage. The windows here are wider than the more common Georgian examples with four panes across in each of the sliding sashes. The slated roof has a cornice-shaped eaves supported on projecting brackets.

25. Two-storey House, Castle Street, Eighteenth Century

During the nineteenth century the symmetrical, brick street elevation of the house and shop on Castle Street was amended with the inclusion of a shopfront and an additional door. Initially the ground level had a central doorcase with a pair of standard Georgian six-pane windows on either side. The doorcase featured a panel door flanked by fluted side columns with a radial arrange fanlight. The fanlight was framed with a moulded arch and a wedged keystone. Immediately overhead was an open base triangular pediment. The building once acted as a grammar school and during the nineteenth century the house was partially converted to business use. During this period the window to the left of the doorcase was replaced by a shop window. This featured a pattern of Georgian panes with fluted reveals and a moulded fascia. Immediately beside the shop window, a doorway to the business unit was inserted with a partially

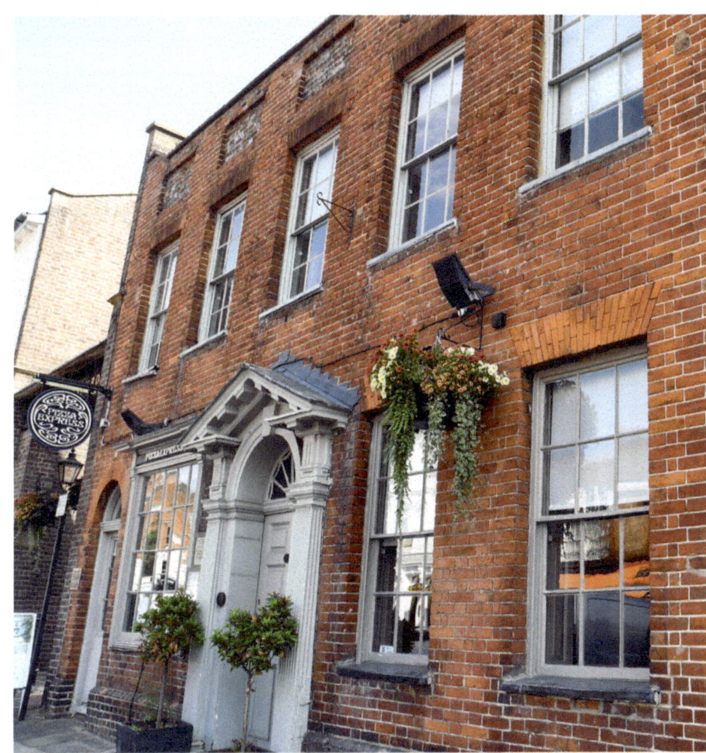

The two-storey brick house and shop on Castle Street has a central doorcase and an arrangement of Georgian windows on the ground and first floors in addition to a pair of dormer windows on the hipped, tiled roof – a ground-floor shop window and side door were added to this.

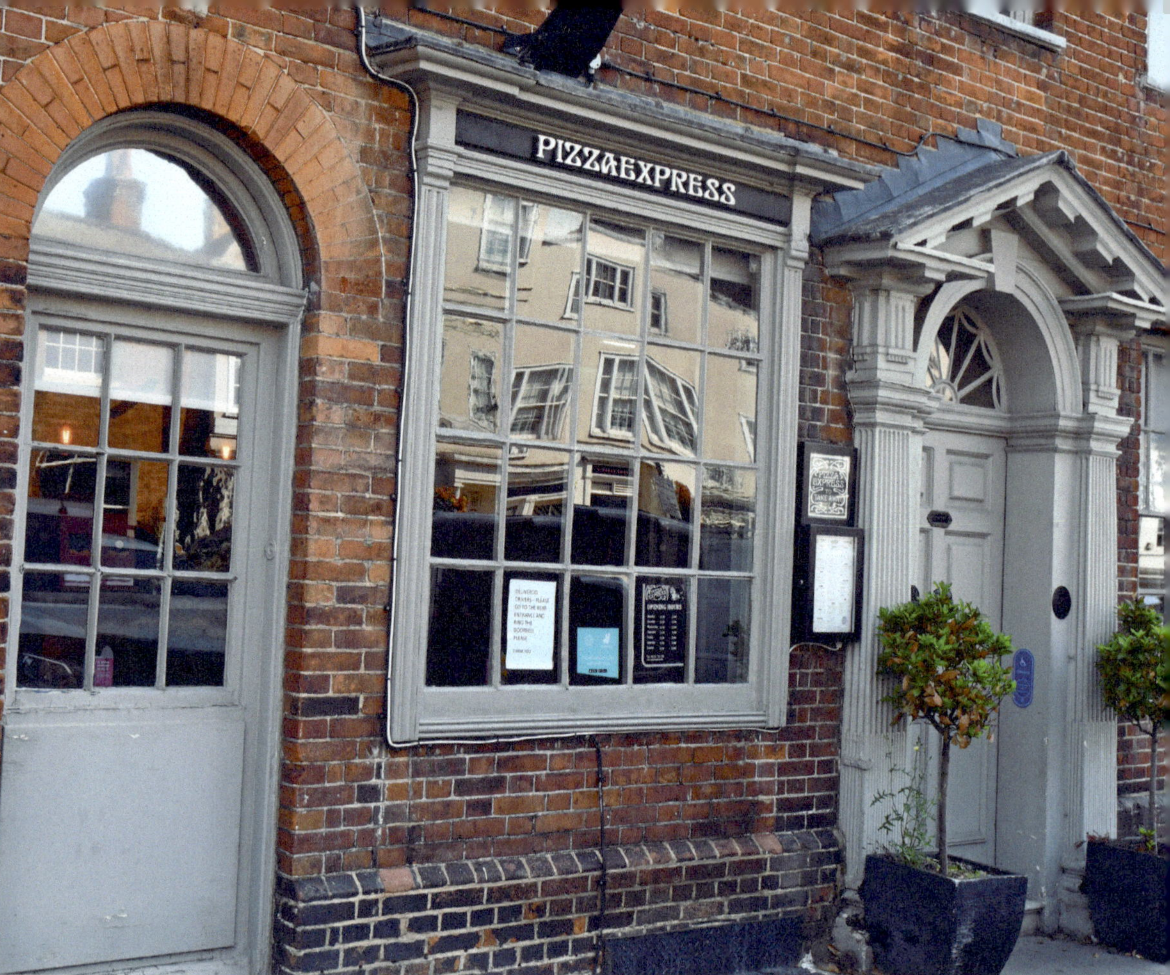

The additional door and display window added to one side of the two-storey house on Castle Street during the nineteenth century.

glazed door and a semicircular fanlight. On the upper level, the five Georgian windows match those of the remaining ground-level windows, while overhead the parapet has five recessed dark brick panels positioned directly over the first-floor windows. Overhead, the tiled hipped roof has two Georgian-style six-pane dormer windows.

26. Two-storey Rendered Houses, Castle Street, Eighteenth Century

The two-storey partially rendered and partially painted brickwork house on Castle Street is one of an identical semi-detached mirrored pair that form part of a continuous streetscape of mixed terraced houses. This has single window on each floor level, a doorway to one side and a tiled roof. The ground-floor window is a twelve-pane Georgian sliding sash, while the upper-level window has two six-pane casement sashes. The four-panel door is linked to the doorway of the adjoining house and has framed surround and a flat moulded hood.

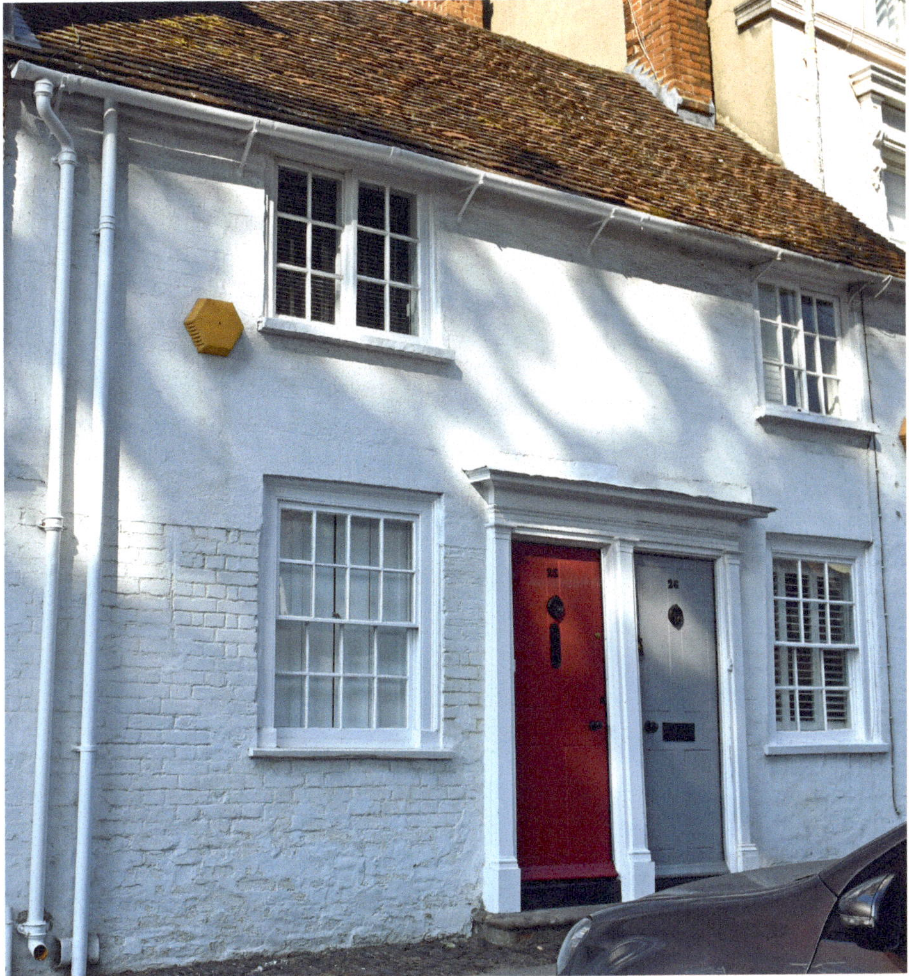

The two-storey rendered house on Castle Street has a window and a doorway to one side and a single window on the first floor.

27. Two-storey House, Castle Street, Eighteenth Century

The two-storey brick symmetrical house on Castle Street dates from the eighteenth century. The ground floor has a central doorway with a Georgian window on each side. The six-panel door has plain reveals, a decorated semicircular fanlight, and an open base triangular pediment with a projecting brick stringcourse on either side of the pediment. The windows have sixteen panes each. The first floor has three Georgian windows: a central twelve pane example and two wider windows similar in scale and directly above the ground-floor windows. An unusual feature of the house is the louvered shutters on each side of the first-floor windows and the tilted eaves that project forward on paired brackets.

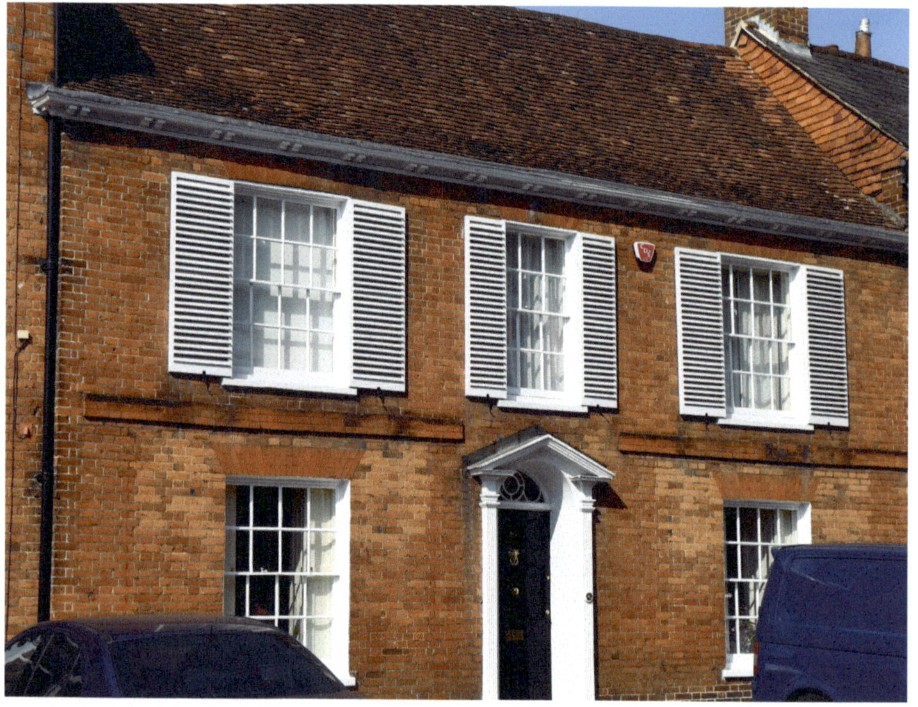

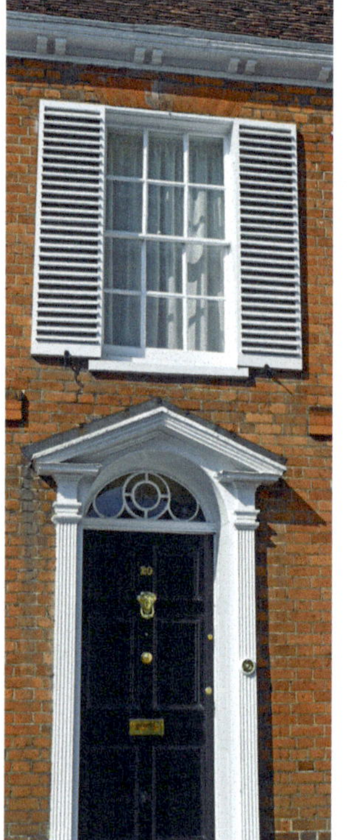

Above: The symmetrical two-storey brick house on Castle Street dates from the eighteenth century.

Left: The panelled door, decorated fanlight, open base pediment, and shuttered window mark the central point of the two-storey house on Castle Street.

28. The Rectory, Upper Church Lane, Eighteenth Century

This two-storey building on Upper Church Lane dates from the eighteenth century and consists of an independent double-storey brick house with an attic storey, four windows and a doorway at ground level and five windows at the first-floor level. The standard Georgian sliding windows have twelve panes, exposed box frames and a cambered heads. A prominent feature of the elevation is the centrally position open porch that dates from the nineteenth century. Here the panelled door has a moulded surround, an arched opening, a plain fanlight, and a tall gabled roof. This is projected outwards on a pair of brackets, immediately above which is a painted stringcourse that marks the level of the first floor. Access to the doorway is provided by a flight of stone steps. The gabled tiled roof has a moulded eaves carried on scrolled brackets, above which are a pair of dormer casement windows with tile hung gables that also date from the twentieth century. The house has a single- and double-storey brick extension, which were both added in the early years of the twentieth century.

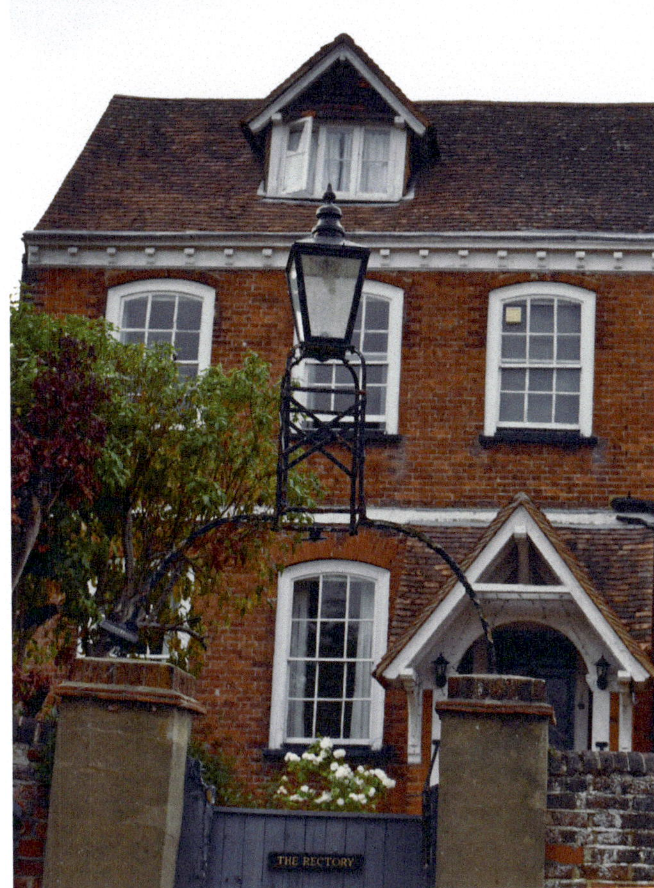

The double-storey, brick Rectory on Upper Church Lane has ten Georgian windows, a gabled porch and attic dormer windows.

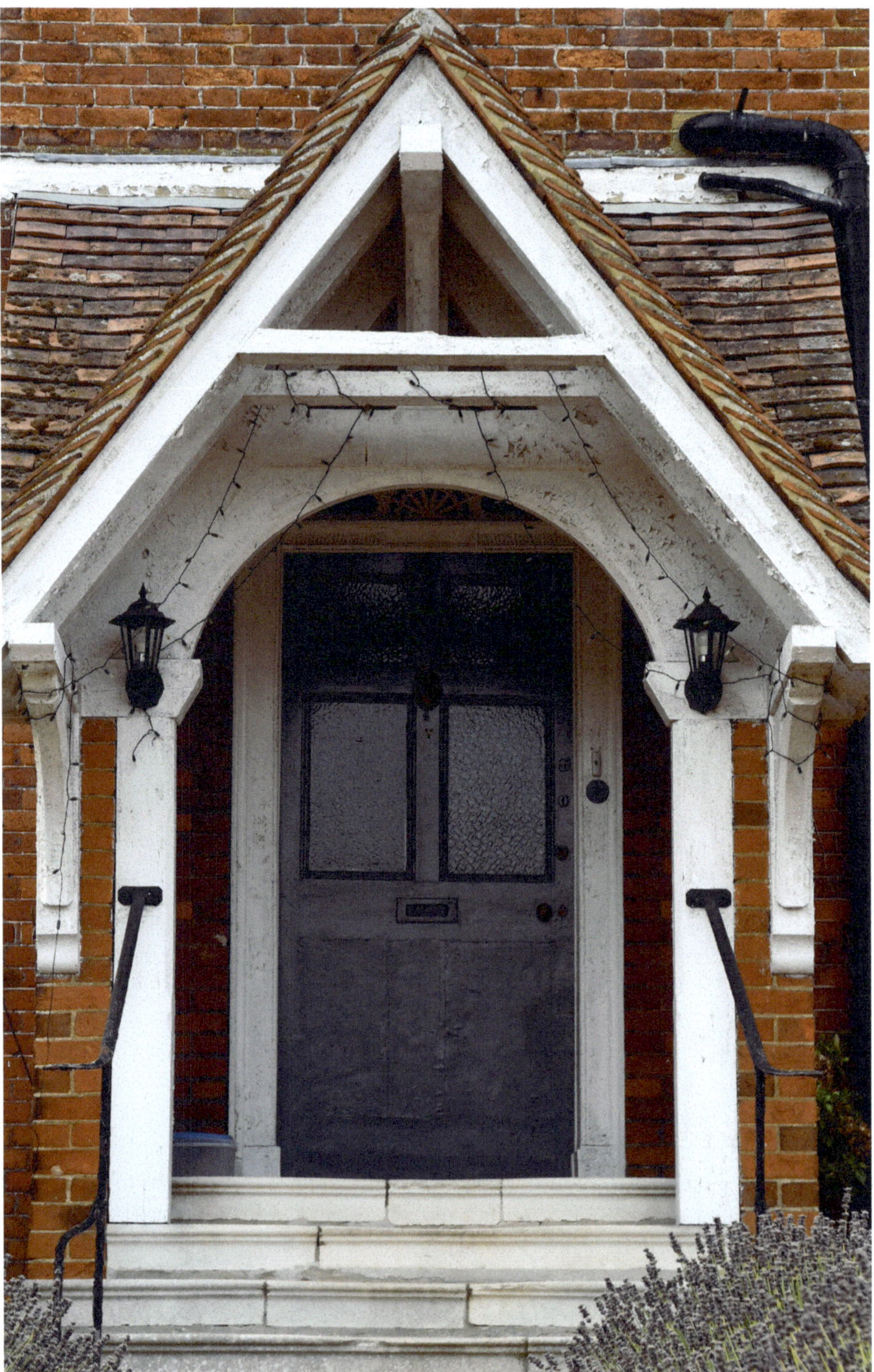

The impressive porch of the Rectory on Upper Church Lane has a tall open gable on projecting brackets.

Farnham Library, originally Vernon House, on West Street is U-shaped in layout with a two-storey central block and flanking side wings on either side that enclose a landscape courtyard that opens onto West Street. The building has a complex history, parts of which dates from the seventeenth century, or earlier, although the date of 1727 on the rainwater pipes suggest that most of the building dates from the eighteenth century. The two-storey rendered library building has a tiled, hipped roof, partially screened behind the plain parapet with its stone coping. The street-facing doorcase in the centre of the main block opens onto the courtyard and is flanked on either side by a single Georgian window, while overhead three similar first-floor windows are spaced across the elevation to line up with the pattern of the doorway and windows of the ground level. The panelled door has plain reveals, side columns and a triangular pediment opened at the base. The windows of the flanking side blocks are arranged with two Georgian windows on each level, one above the other, so that all the windows of the building face onto the courtyard. The courtyard itself is paved in a circular pattern with stone sets and separated from the street by a plain metal railing. This has a decorated, arched opening with a central lamp. An interesting note relating to the house is that Charles I stayed here on the way to his trial and execution in 1649.

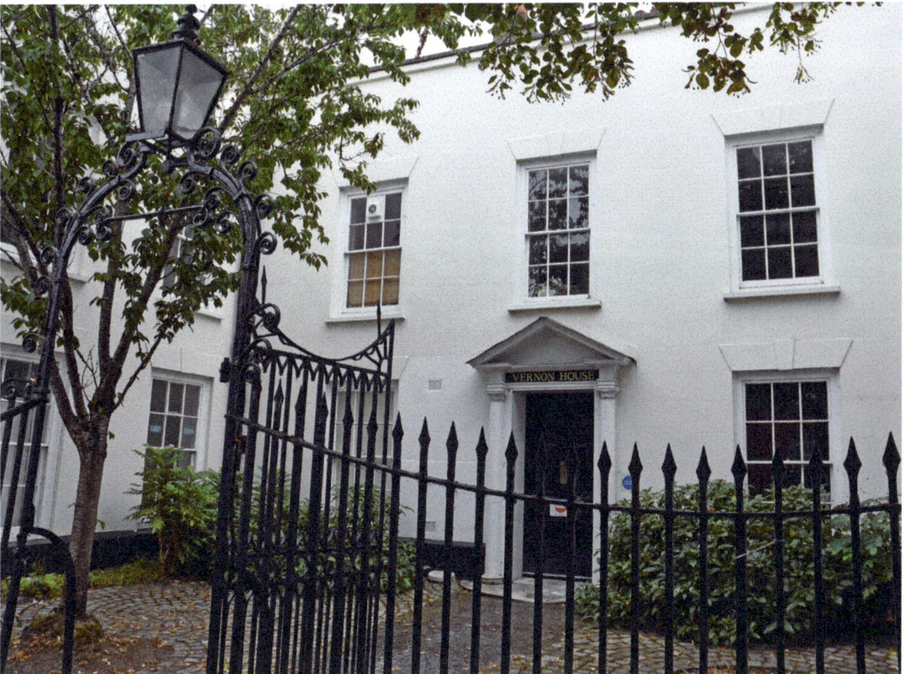

The double-storey Farnham Library building is U-shaped in layout and faces onto West Street.

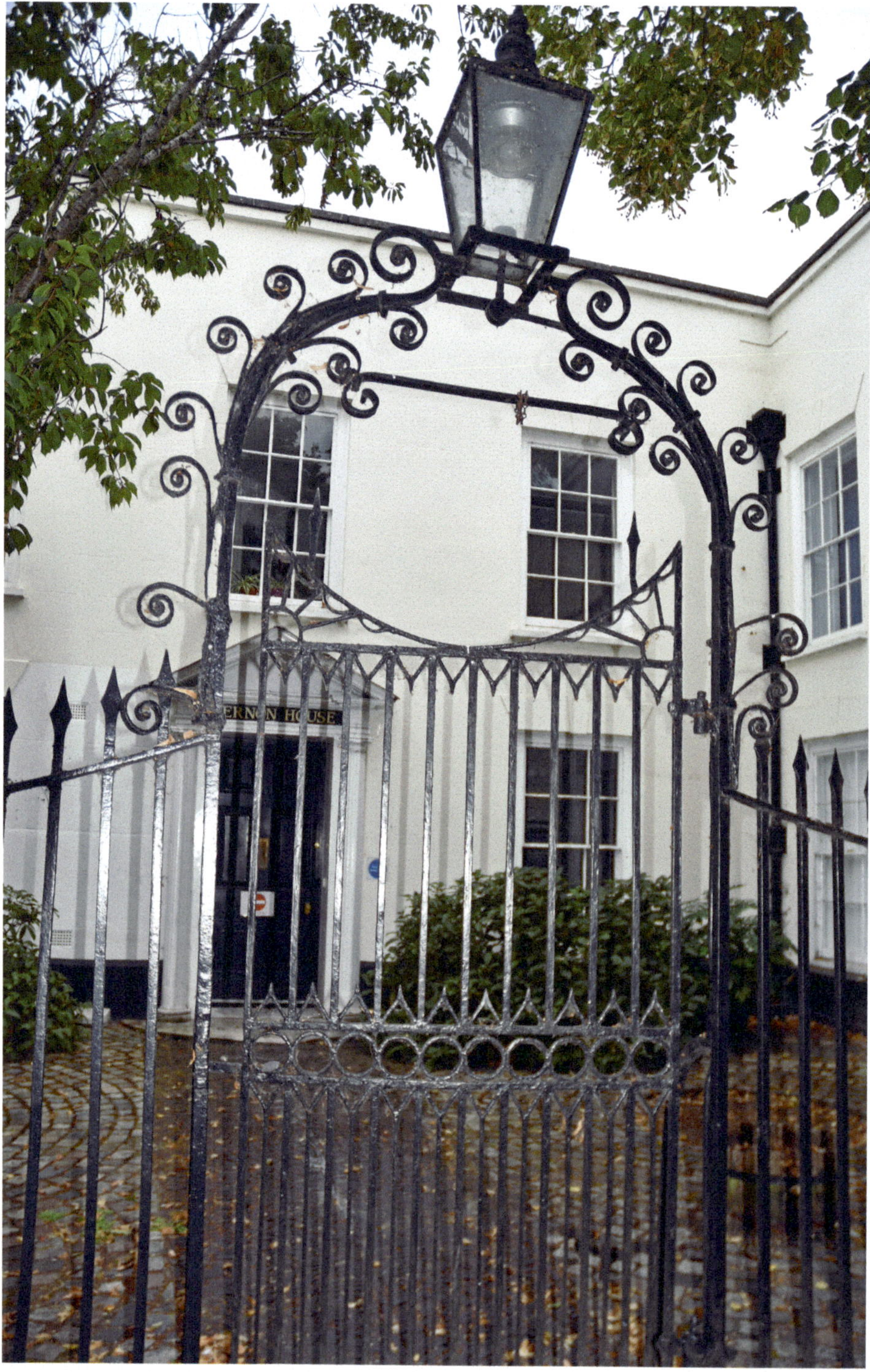

The metal front railings and archway of Farnham Library separates the courtyard from West Street.

30. Sandford House, West Street, 1757

The impressive Sandford House dates from 1757 and is one of a group of large houses in this section of West Street. The brick house is three storeys high, with the three floor levels defined by two moulded stringcourses and a central projecting bay. The narrow central bay features a ground-level doorcase and a single window on the first- and second-floor levels and a triangular dental pediment. The elaborate doorcase has a panelled door with a cambered fanlight set into a rusticated back-panelled archway, which includes a wedge-shaped keystone and flat, fluted side columns that support an open base triangular pediment. Overhead, each of the upper-floor levels have a single camber-headed Georgian window with

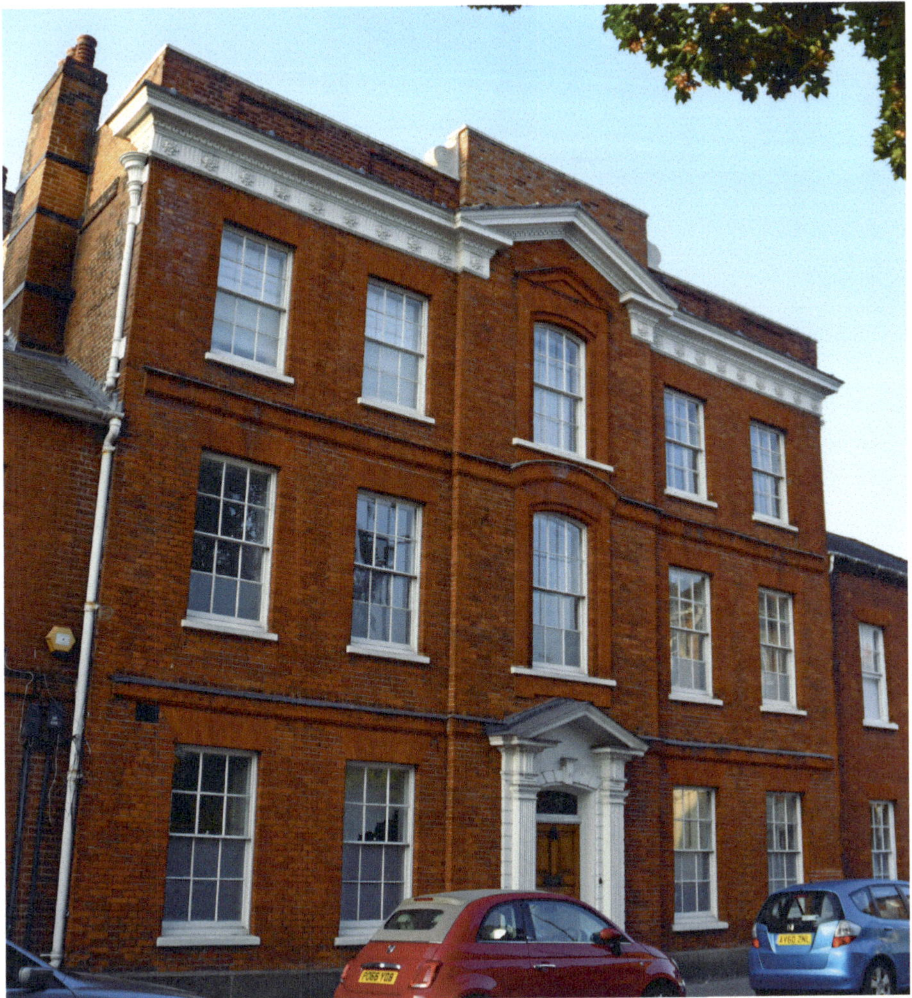

The three-storey brick Sandford House on West Street features and arrangement of Georgian windows, a central bay and doorway and an elaborate roofline cornice.

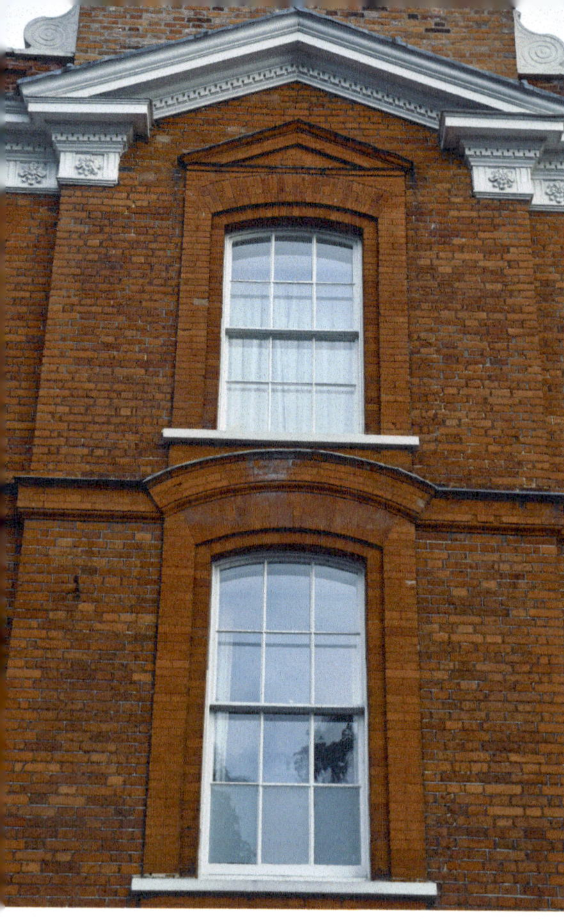

The central bay of Sandford House on West Street has a central doorcase, camber-headed windows on the two upper floors and an open base triangular pediment – all aligned one above the other.

brick architraves and heads on each floor. Elsewhere the side bays on either side of the projecting bay have two standard twelve-pane Georgian sashes on each level. Across the roofline is an elaborate moulded painted cornice, above which the brick parapet has recessed panelling.

31. Bathune House, West Street, Eighteenth Century

Bathune House on West Street is a large brick house with a basement on West Street that dates from around 1780. The symmetrical house is three storeys high with a central doorcase and two flanking windows at ground level, five windows evenly spaced across the front on the first- and second-floor levels and the tip of two basement windows extending above the footpath level. The standard Georgian windows on all three levels have sliding sashes with twelve panes. The elaborate doorcase has a six-panelled door, radiating style fanlight, an arch, framed side panels, fluted columns with decorated heads, and an open base triangular pediment. The roofline is marked by a moulded stringcourse on brackets with a plain brick parapet overhead that effectively screens the gabled roof. The later two-storey extension to the left side is similar in design with Georgian windows and an arched doorcase.

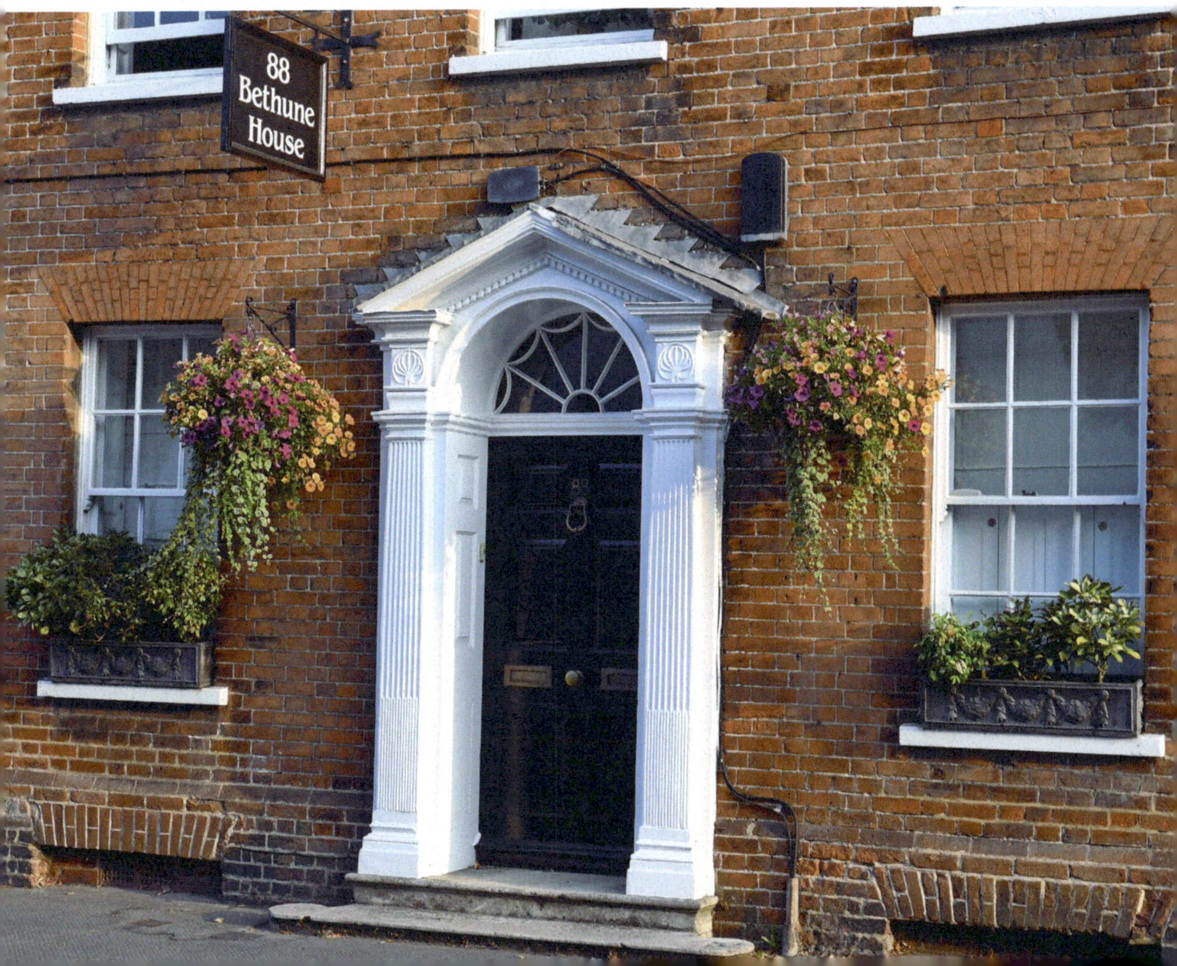

Right: Bathune House is one of the large, symmetrical, brick houses on West Street with Georgian windows, a moulded stringcourse and a central doorcase.

Below: The central striking doorcase of Bathune House on West Street has a panelled door, radial fanlight, framed side panels, fluted uprights, and an open base triangular pediment.

32. Individual House, Castle Street, Eighteenth Century

The individual house on Castle Street was built by Thomas Piggott and is one of the few houses to have been provided with a landscaped front garden, to which an ornamental metal gate set between brick piers with ball-topped finials provides access from the street. The house is two storey high over a basement and includes a front porch, a tiled hipped roof with a wide eaves, and a painted and moulded stringcourse at mid-level. The house has four standard Georgian sash windows on the basement and ground level, with five similar windows on the upper floor and a slated roof. The central placed open entrance porch has a pair of circular columns that support a moulded flat roof. This is approached by seven stone moulded steps with metal guard rails on either side. The entrance door beyond is framed by flat, fluted side frames while the double door is divided into two sets of panels, with a projecting lamp on the upper frame.

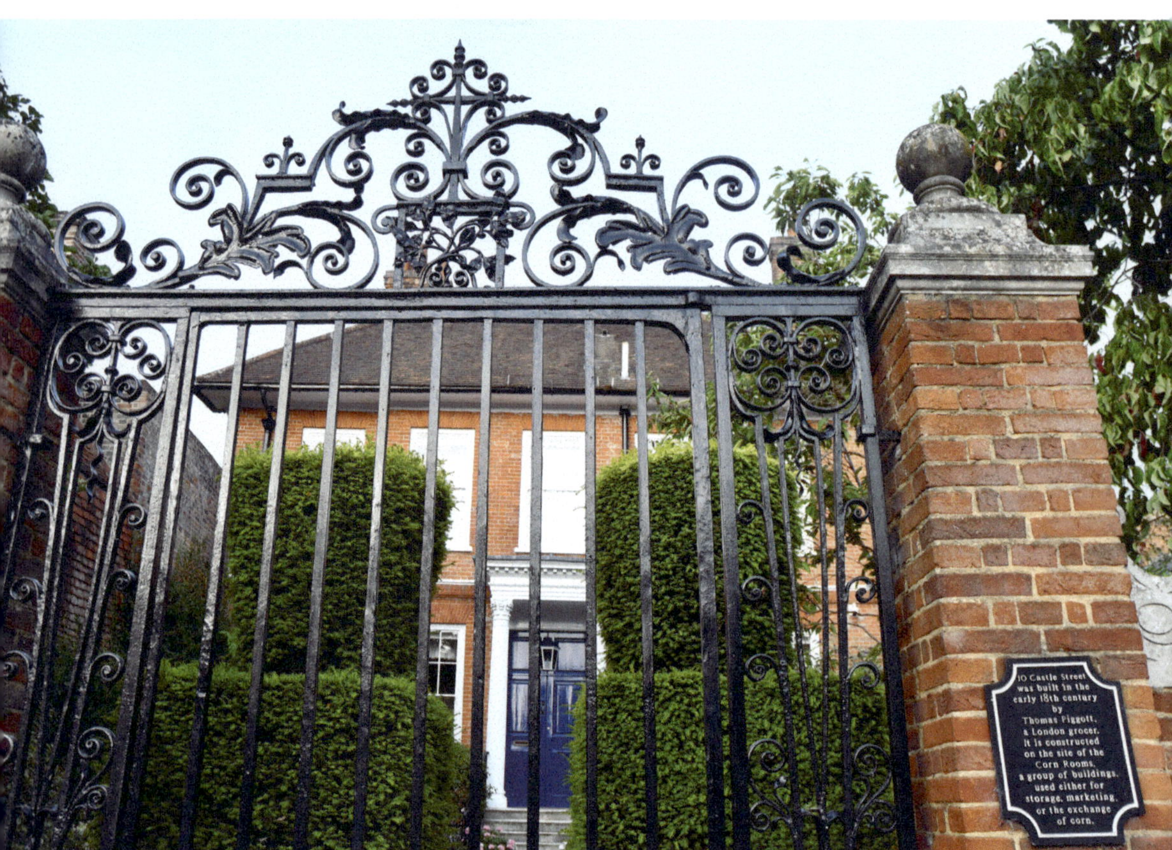

The landscaped front garden to the individual house on Castle Street has ornamental gates and brick piers with ball-topped finials.

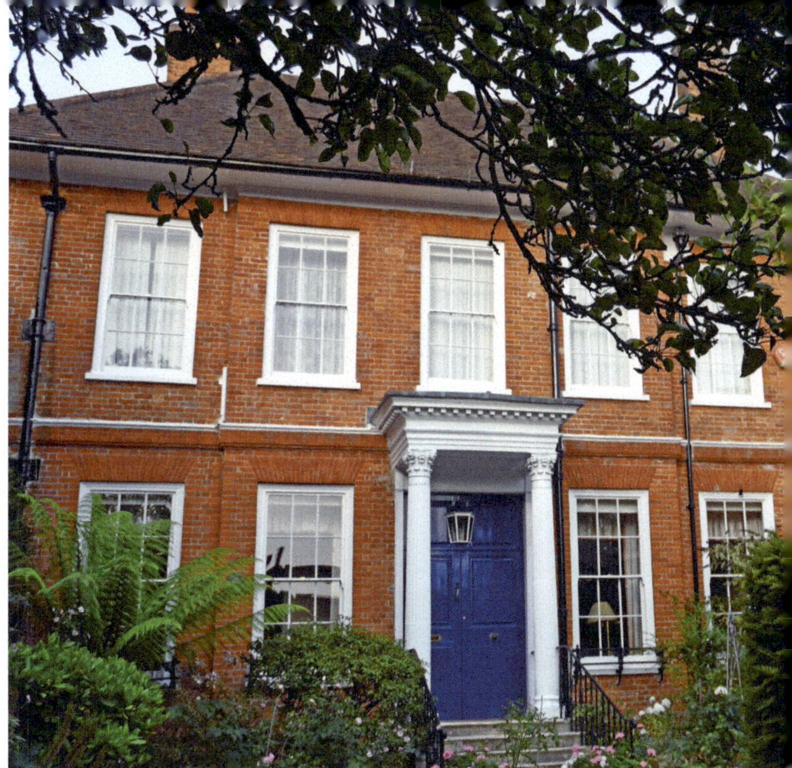

The two-storey individual brick house on Castle Street features a front porch, Georgian windows and a hipped roof.

33. Two-storey Linked Brick House, West Street, 1790

One of a pair of two-storey linked brick houses on West Street built in 1790, according to a date on the drainpipe. The house on the left is two storeys in height with an attic storey and a basement and is the narrower of two. The houses were only linked together around 1900 when a narrow, recessed bay was inserted between the two gables. This is similar in height to the houses, with a plain arched accessed door to the rear and a blank brick window-sized opening at first-floor level. The house has a doorcase on the right-hand side at ground level. This is beside the narrow bay arched door and flanked on the left by a pair of standard Georgian windows. The first floor has three similar windows aligned on the two ground-floor windows and the entrance door. Initially the house had an open area at basement level, with two windows opening onto the low-level area. However, like many Farnham houses this area was filled in and incorporated into the footpath at some time in the past, so that today all the remains are the heads of the basement windows that protrude above the footpath level. The elaborate doorcase follows the common Farnham arrangement. This includes a panelled door, framed surrounds, fluted side columns, an arched fanlight with radial glazing, and an open base triangular pediment. Immediately beside the stone steps is a cast-iron foot scraper. The house also features a tiled roof, a painted stringcourse that stretches above the ground-floor window heads, a moulded cornice above the first-floor windows, and a brick parapet, above which the two flat-headed dormer casement sashes are visible.

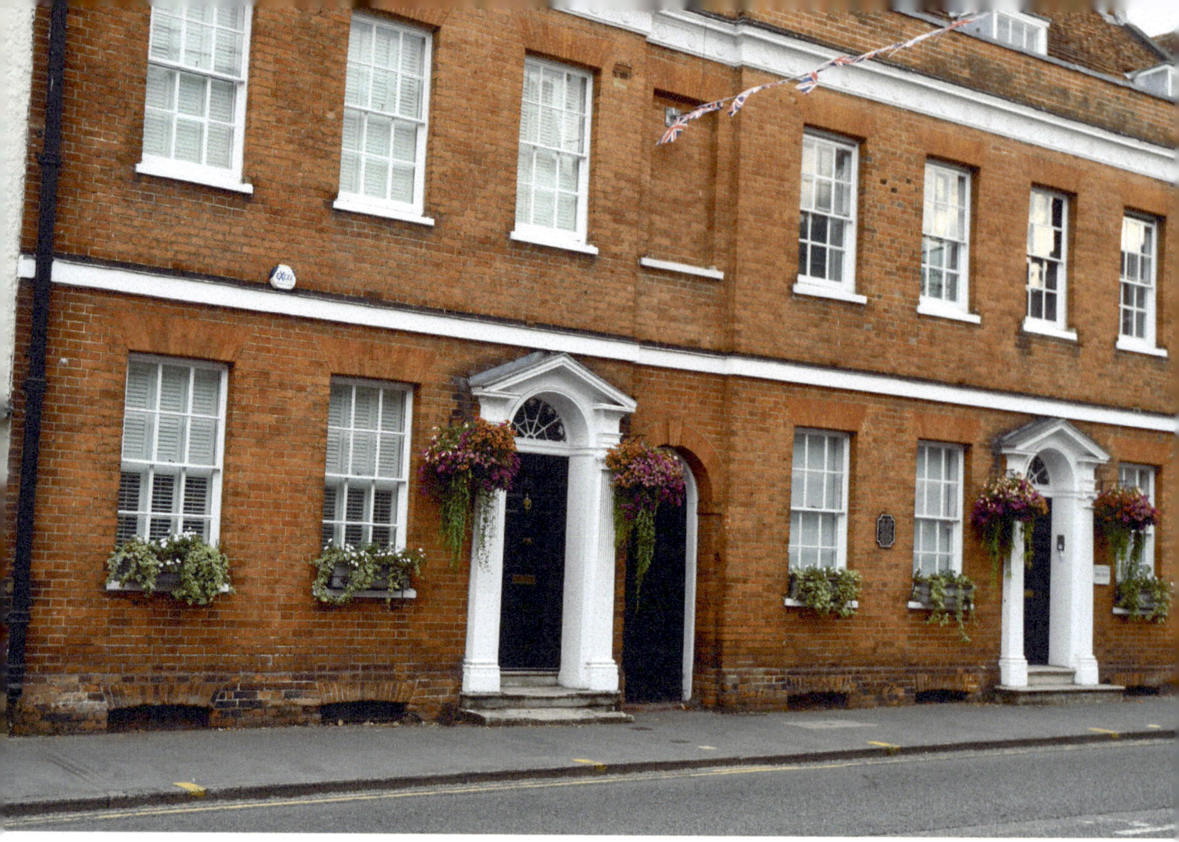

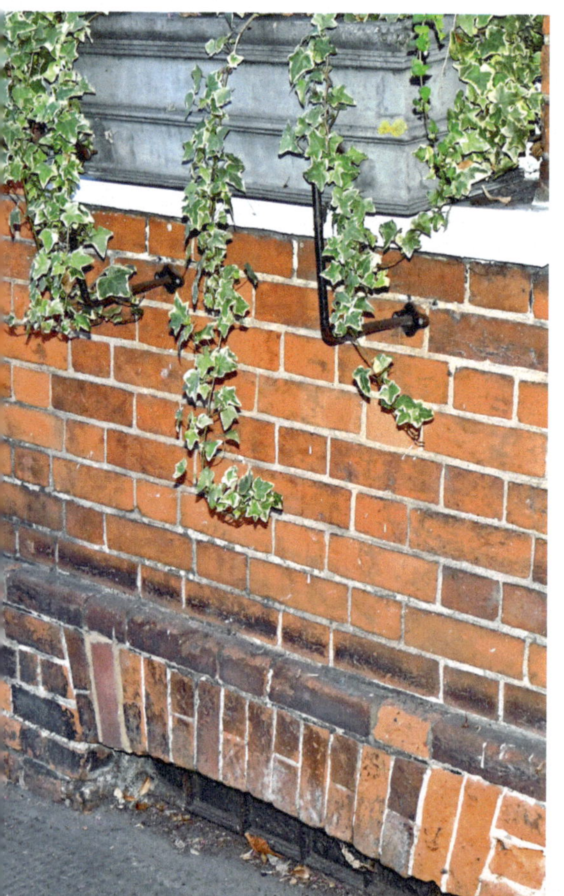

Above: The two-storey brick house on West
Street has five Georgian windows, a framed
doorcase to one side and a stepped-back link to
the adjoining similar house.

Left: The head of the basement window
protrudes above the line of the footpath,
subsequent to the basement area having been
filled in and incorporated into it.

34. End Cottage, West Street, Eighteenth Century

The brick, two-storey, end-of-terrace cottage on West Street is one of a group of terraced cottages on West Street. This has a single window at ground level and the door to one side, in addition to a single window on the first-floor level. The ground-floor window has a camber head with two casement sashes, each casement divided into six panes. The first-floor window is not dissimilar, but has a flat head

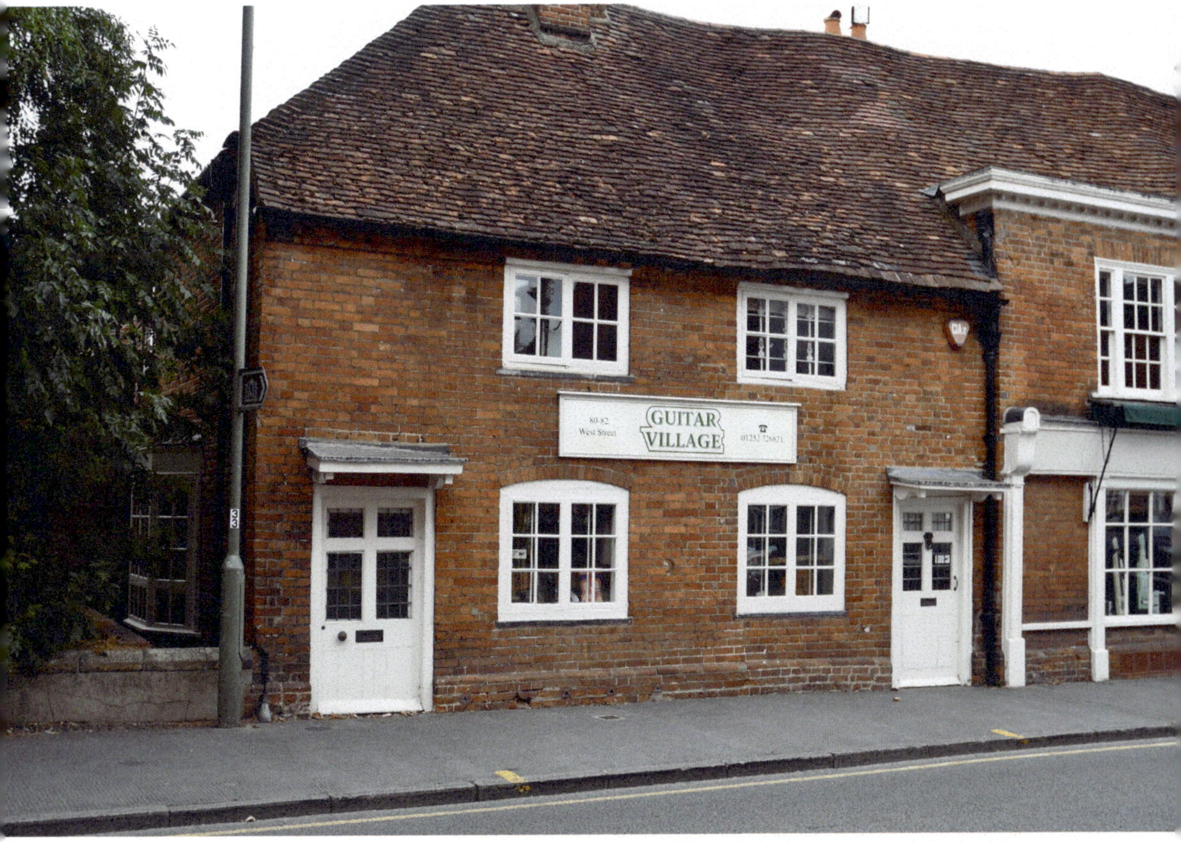

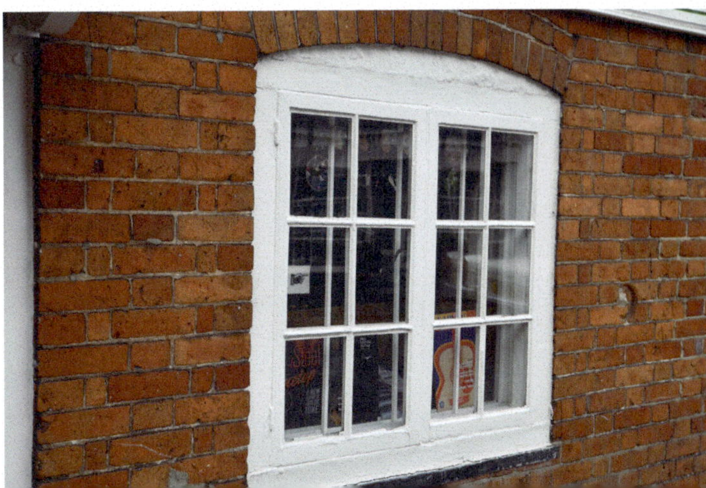

Above: The brick, two-storey, end-of-terrace cottage on West Street has a single window on the ground and first floor and the entrance door to one side.

Right: The camber-headed ground-floor casement windows of the end cottage on West Street.

directly below the eaves of the steep tiled hipped roof. This also has two casement sashes, but here the sashes have four panes. The panelled door to one side has glazed leaded panels on the upper section, a plain surround and a projecting hood carried on curved brackets.

35. Nelson Arms, Castle Street, Eighteenth Century

The Nelson Arms Pub on Castle Street is a wide pebble-dashed building on the corner of Park Row. The pub was in the past named the Hand and the Pen and the Bakers Arms in the eighteenth century and acquired the Nelson Arms name in the nineteenth century. The building dates from the eighteenth century and consisted initially of three bays, with the pub confined to the left-hand bay. Later the pub use was extended to include the full width of the block and the elevation was amended. So that today the extended pebble-dashed rustic-looking building is two storeys high with an arrangement of different window forms and a continuous tiled roof. The ground-floor level has a complex arrangement of two doorways

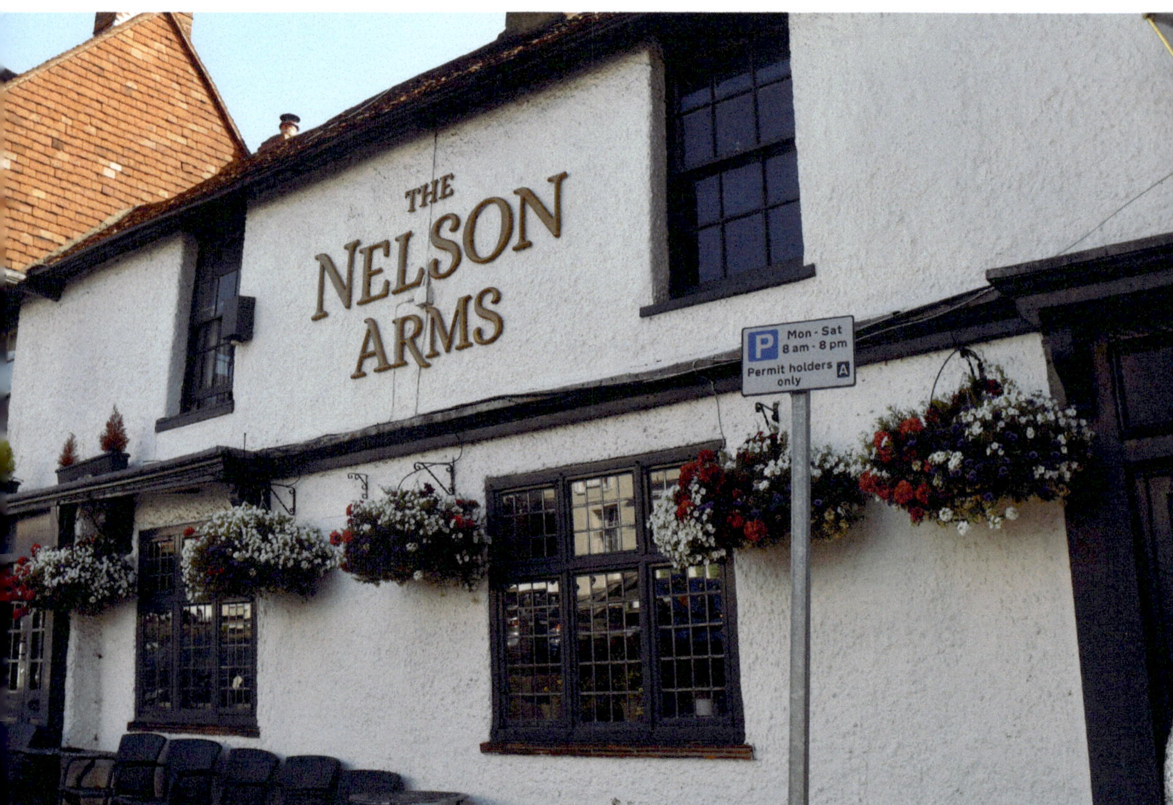

The two-storey, pebble-dashed Nelson Arms on Castle Street.

and three windows. The two entrance doors are similarly arranged: one near the left side of the building, the other on the right-hand corner with Park Row. These feature double doors with glazed panes, plain side columns, a blank fanlight, a projecting overhead hood with projecting brackets and an overhead hanging sign above the left doorway. There is also a painted stringcourse linking the hoods of the doorways together. The ground-level windows have six sashes each with mullion and transom framing and leaded casements, while the projecting and splayed left end window has ten sashes also with mullion and transom framing, and leaded casements. The first-floor window arrangement is different and includes three standard Georgian windows spaced irregularly across the front.

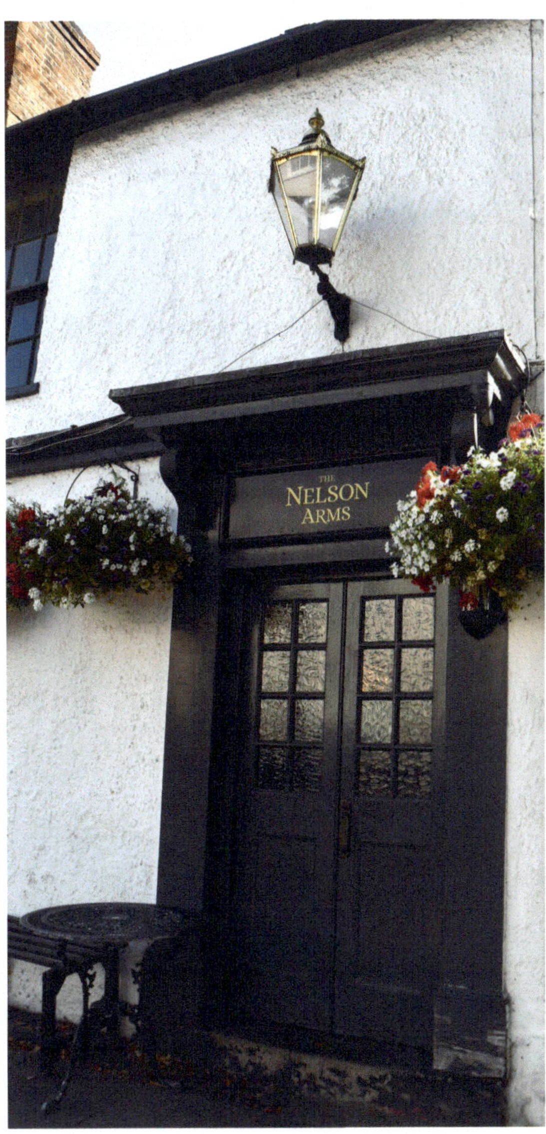

The half-glazed entrance doorways to the Nelson Arms on Castle Street have double doors with blank fan sashes, side columns and projecting heads.

36. Bishop's Table Hotel, West Street, 1750

The Bishop's Table Hotel on West Street is an extremely long two-storey house with Georgian windows. The block is rendered with a hipped roof, a stone coped parapet, a coach arch to one side and a projecting bay with the entrance doorcase. The standard Georgian sliding sash windows – six on the ground level and seven on the upper level – have twelve panes and moulded architraves, except for the single window on the projecting bay. This is Palladian in form with the central sash flanked on either side by much narrow sashes. The hipped roof has three flat-headed leaded dormer windows irregularly spaced across the roofline. The central panelled door on the projecting bay is set into a miniature triumphal arch. This includes framed side columns, a semicircular fanlight with a glazed lamp, an overhead arch, and a flat moulded head. On the left end is a

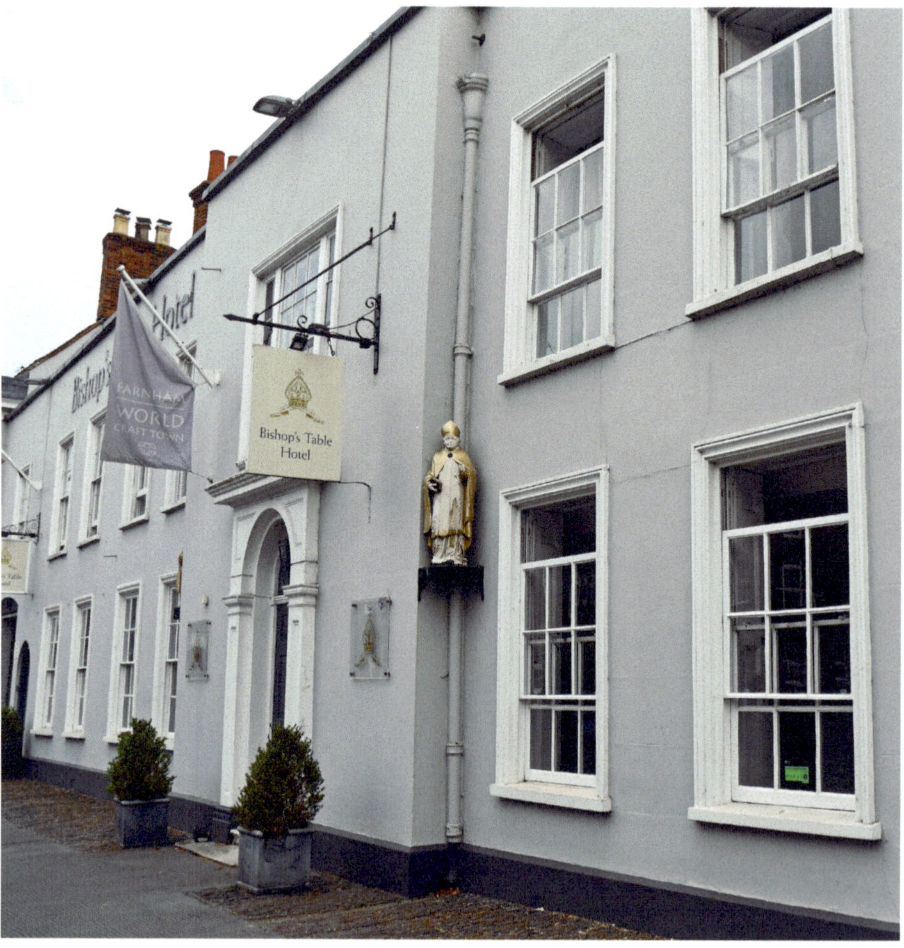

The extended two-storey, rendered elevation of Bishop's Table Hotel, West Street, includes standard Georgian windows and a projecting entrance bay.

cambered coach arch, beside which is a panelled service door with a decorated semicircular fanlight. A curious feature of the elevation is the carved ecclesiastical figures set on brackets into each inner corners of the projecting bay – a reference to hotel name. The hotel had a range of uses in the past including a house and an ecclesiastical school.

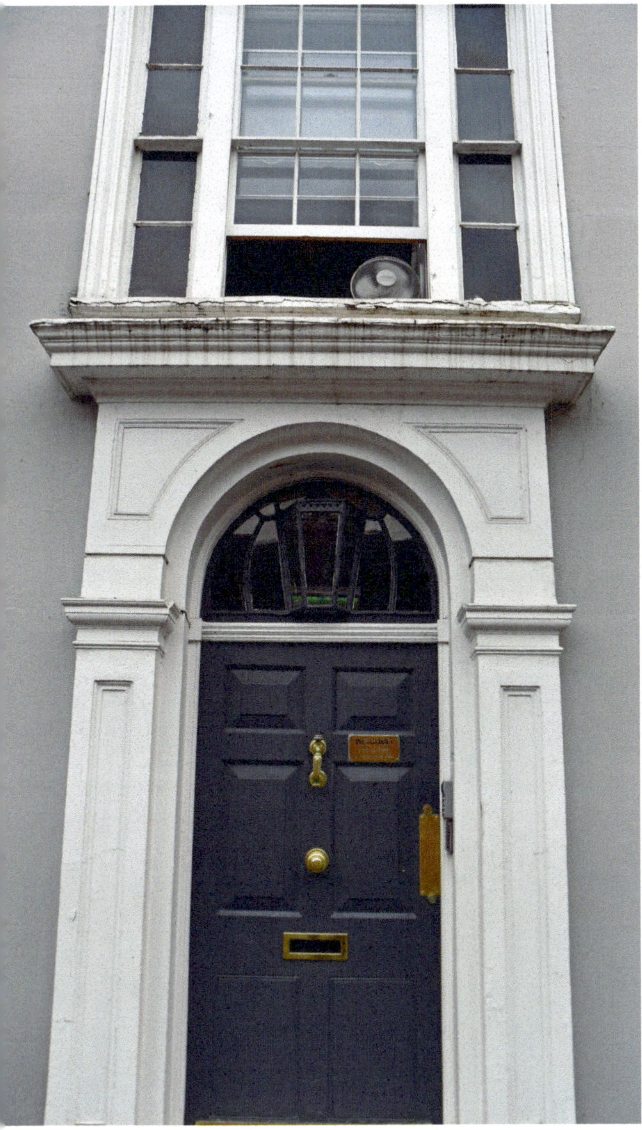

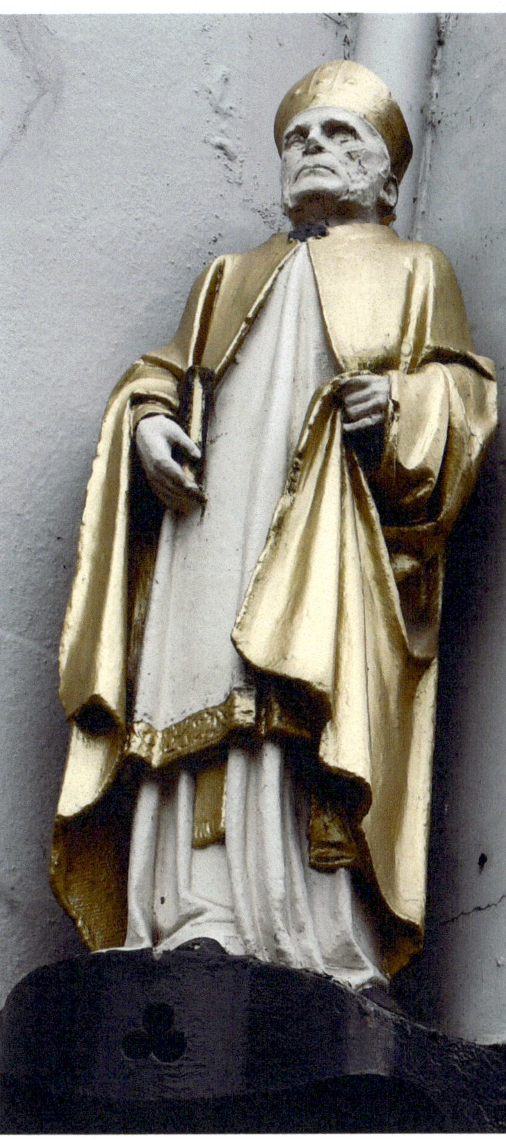

Above left: The arched doorcase, panelled door, fanlight with lantern, framed side columns and Palladian windows of the Bishop's Table Hotel, West Street.

Above right: The carved three-dimensional image of the ecclesiastical figure on the inner corner of the projecting bay of the Bishop's Table Hotel, West Street.

37. Two-storey Corner House, West Street, Nineteenth Century

The two-storey brick house on the corner of West Street and the Hart was built as an addition to the adjoining eighteenth-century house during the nineteenth century. This has a slim bay to one side with a doorway and a wider projecting bay on the other corner side with two tripartite windows and a curved and decorated moulded gable. The ground-level doorway is fitted into the slim bay and consists of a panelled door with a glazed oval panel, wide moulded side columns and a triangular pediment. The flat-headed ground-level tripartite window is Palladian in style with three sliding sashes: a wide central sash flanked on either side by narrower sashes. The central sash has twelve panes in contrast to the side sashes which have eight panes. In a similar way, the overhead first-floor Palladian window also has wide central sash flanked by slimmer side sashes. The distinguishing feature of the first-floor window, however, is the taller central sash which has a semicircular head beneath a brick arch.

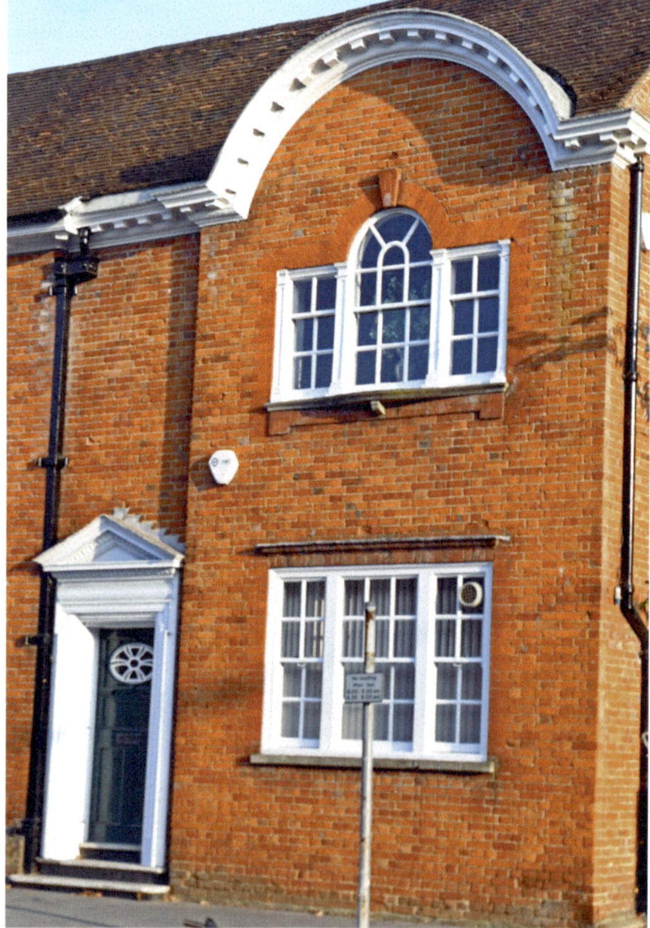

The double-storey corner house on West Street features Palladian windows and a pronounced curved gable.

38. Two-storey Symmetrical House, Downing Street, 1830

The two-storey symmetrical house on Downing Street dates from the eighteenth century, although the current façade dates from around 1830. The form of the house is primarily Georgian but with decorative elements, including strings and architraves. The two-storey elevation is divided into the ground- and upper-floor level by a rendered stringcourse with a further but more elaborate moulded cornice immediately below the plain brick parapet. The ground level has a central doorway flanked on either side by a single Palladian window with wide moulded surrounds. The six-panel door has a semicircular fanlight and a moulded surround, outside of which is an arrangement of stepped stone blocking – all set in a concave

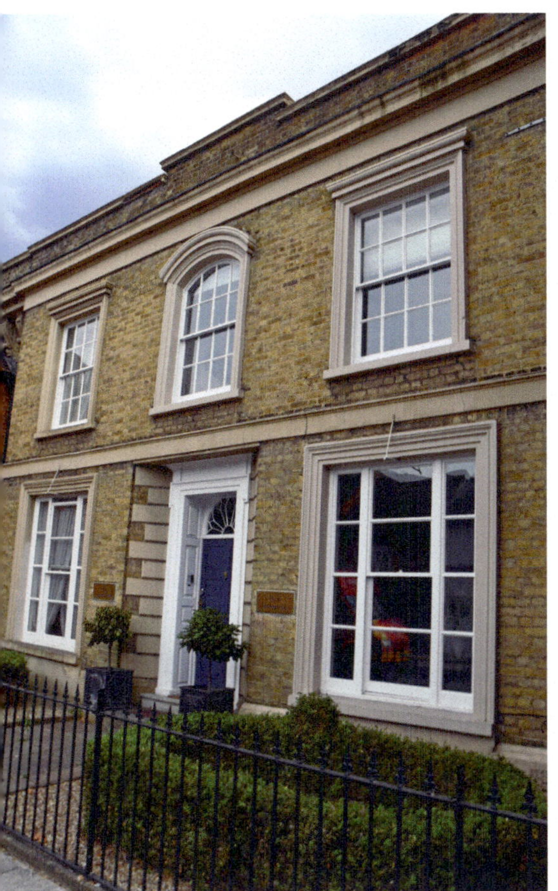 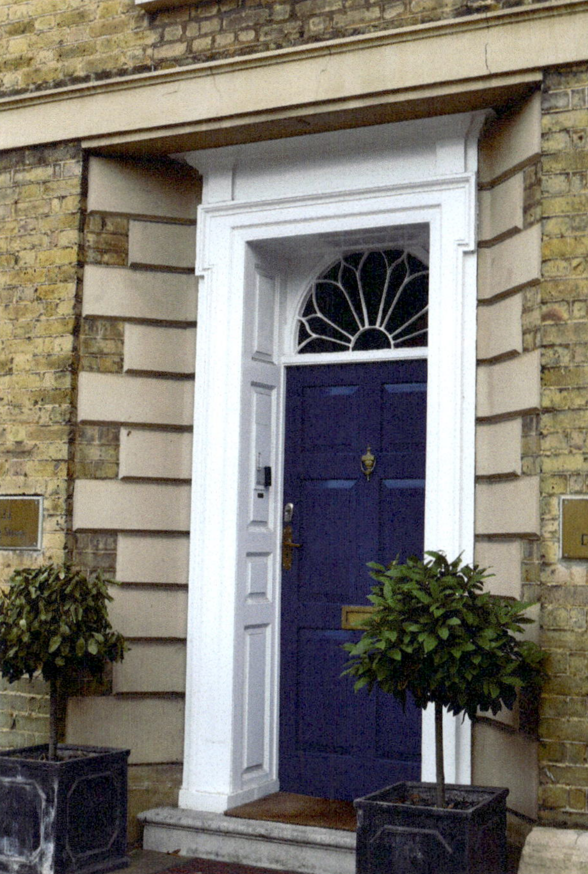

Above left: The two-storey symmetrical house on Downing Street has elaborate decorative elements including moulded strings, moulded surrounds, differing-scale windows, and an elaborate doorcase.

Above right: The doorcase of the house on Downing Street has a panelled door, radial fanlight, moulded surrounds, and stepped blocking, all set in a concave recess.

recess. The first floor has three wide Georgian windows that match the spacing of the ground-floor door and window openings. The central window has a moulded camber head and the side windows have flat moulded heads. An interesting feature of the house is the narrow set back at each end. Each has a pair of brackets directly underneath the line of the upper stringcourse. The house is further unusual in that it has a shallow front garden separated from the footpath by a low metal railing.

39. Merriott House, West Street, 1840

The two-storey rendered Merriott House on West Street dates from the eighteenth century but was rendered around 1840. The house features rusticated rendering at ground level and plain rendering on the first floor. This includes a moulded stringcourse between the ground level and the upper floor and a heavily moulded cornice at the parapet level that partially screens the tiled roof. The ground floor features the doorway to one side flanked by a pair of windows. The elegant doorcase has a panelled door that includes glazed panes on the upper level and an overhead decorated fanlight with circular glazing. This is framed by plain surround

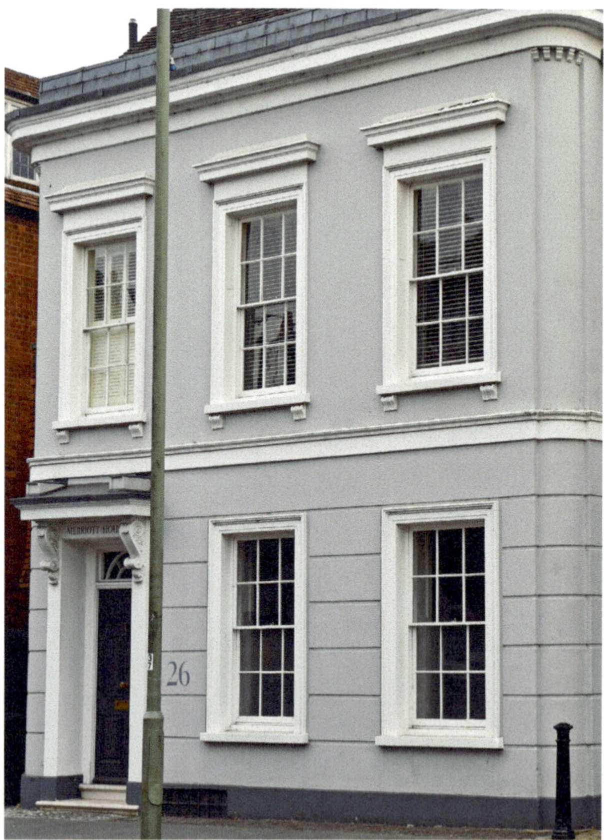

The two-storey Merriott House on West Street with rounded corners, a rusticated ground-level and first-floor rendering.

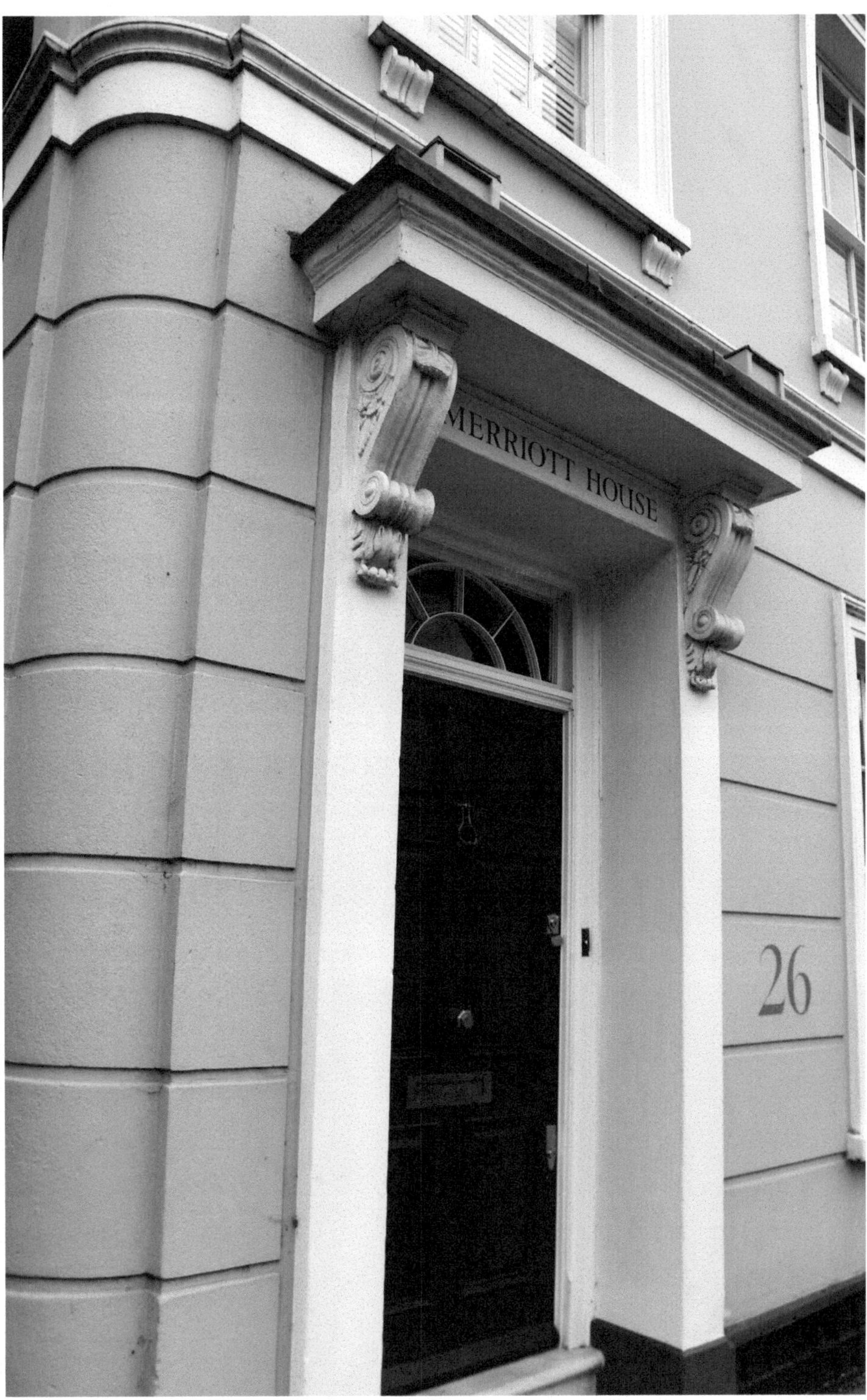

The elaborate doorcase and rounded corners of Merriott House on West Street.

set between squared columns, the heads of which support curved brackets that in turn carry a flat pediment. The standard Georgian sliding windows on both levels are similar with twelve panes and moulded surrounds, in addition to which the three upper-floor windows are equally spaced across the elevation and have undersill brackets and overhead moulded pediments.

40. Three-storey Rendered Houses, Castle Street, 1866

The three-storey houses with a basement on Castle Street is Italianate in style and is part of a group of three similar terraced houses built by F. C. Birch in 1866. The brick house is colour washed with a stringcourse between the first- and

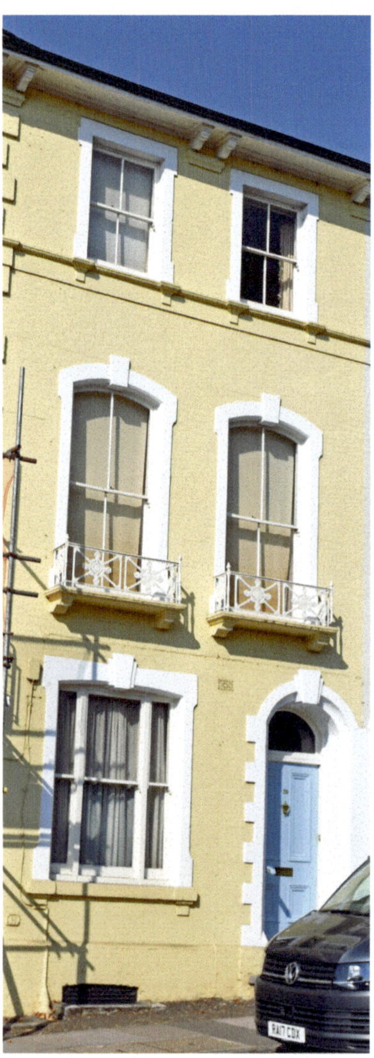

The three-storey, brick, colour-washed house on Castle Street has its doorway to one side, a Palladian window at ground level, a pair of windows on each of the upper levels, and end quoins.

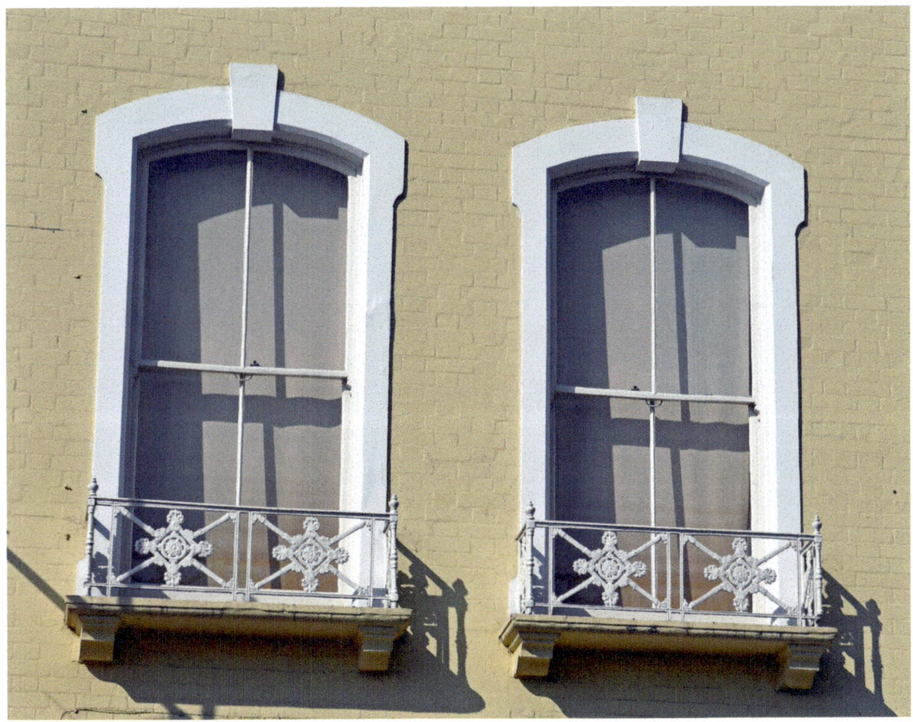

The first-floor windows of the house on Castle Street have sliding sashes with plain surrounds, cambered heads, keystones, and a decorated metal flower guard.

second-floor levels and stepped quoins that mark the end of the terrace. The house has the entrance door to one side, a single window at ground level, and a pair of windows on each of the upper floors. The entrance door has four panels with a plain rendered semicircular fanlight, stepped surround and arch with a keystone. The single Palladian ground-floor window has a central two-pane middle sash, a narrow side sash with two panes and a plain rendered surround with a slightly cambered head and a keystone. The first-floor windows have two large panes in each of the sliding sashes, a plain surround, a cambered head with a wedge-shaped keystone, and a decorated metal flower guard at sill level. The second-floor windows are lower in height. These have four panes in each of the sliding sashes, and a plain surround with slight shouldering. Overhead, the projecting eaves is carried on pairs of brackets.

41. Three-storey House, Castle Street, Nineteenth Century

The rendered three-storey house on Castle Street is one of a pair of semi-detached houses, with a doorway to one side and a single twelve-pane standard Georgian window on each of the three floors. The house dates from the nineteenth century

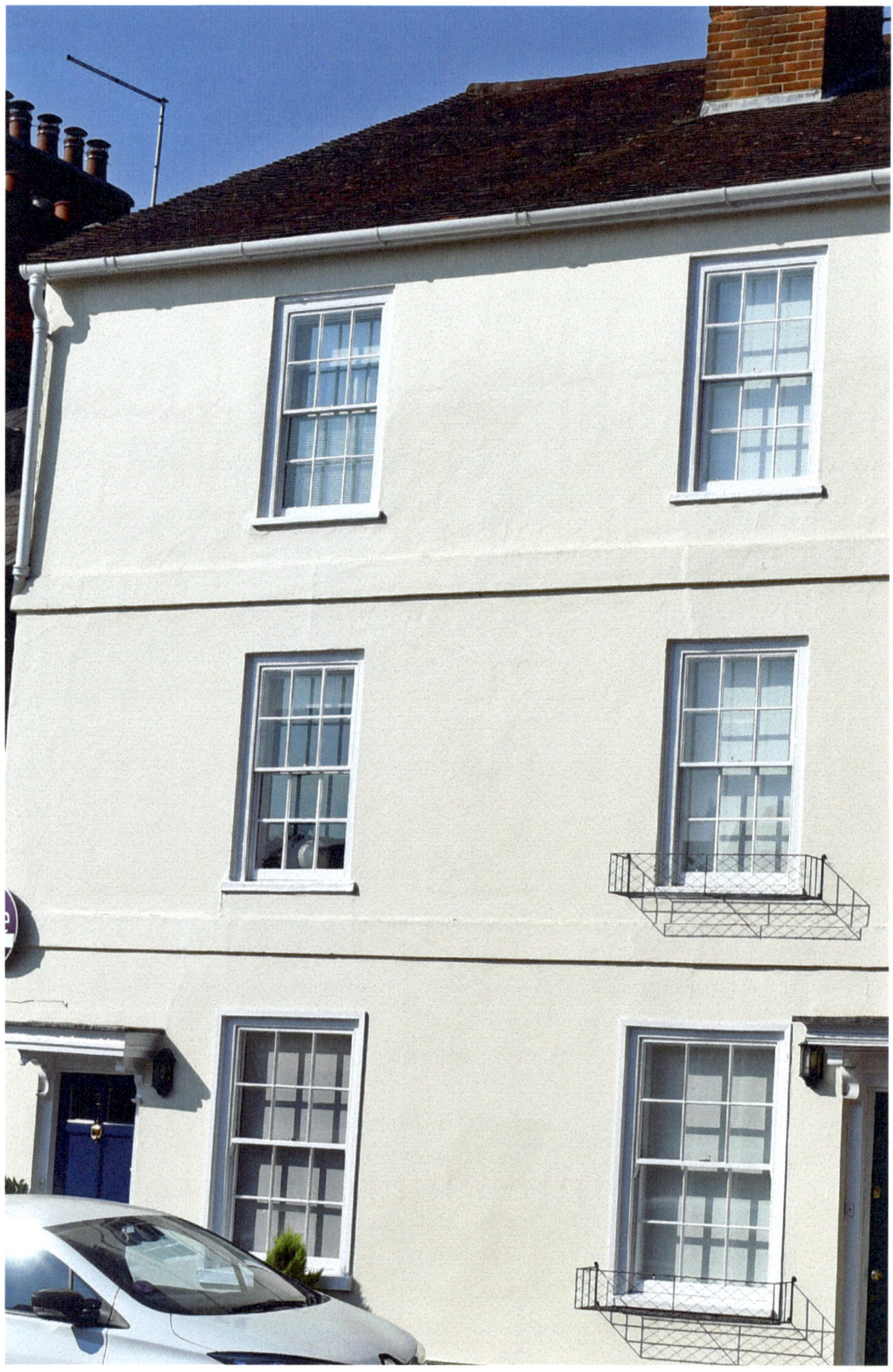

The rendered three-storey house on Castle Street is one of a pair of semi-detatched houses with a doorway to one side and a single standard Georgian window on each of the floors.

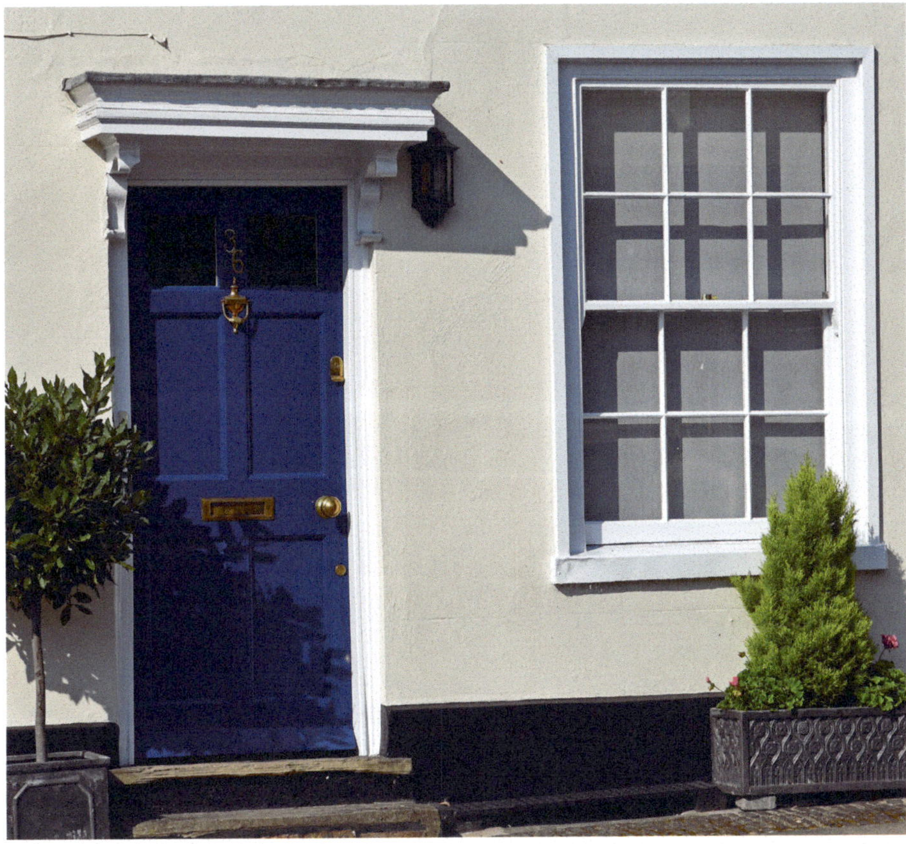

The door to one side of the three-storey house on Castle Street has narrow surrounds and a flat moulded hood carried on projecting brackets.

and has a gabled slated roof and a rendered stringcourse on the first- and second-floor level. The six-panel door to one side has narrow surrounds and a flat moulded hood carried on projecting brackets.

42. Former Castle Inn Building, Castle Street, Nineteenth Century

The three-storey brick building, formerly Castle Inn, on Castle Street has an off-centre doorcase, eleven windows, and a low-pitched slated roof with a moulded cornice and projecting eaves carried on a range of brackets. The doorway has a panelled double door, flanked by narrow round-headed side lights, and an elliptical fanlight with radiating panes. This is set into a stone doorcase with plain side columns, an elliptical arch and a flat hood. The sliding sash Georgian windows are uniformly arranged across the elevation, although they vary in height and widths on the different floor levels. The ground-floor windows have four large panes.

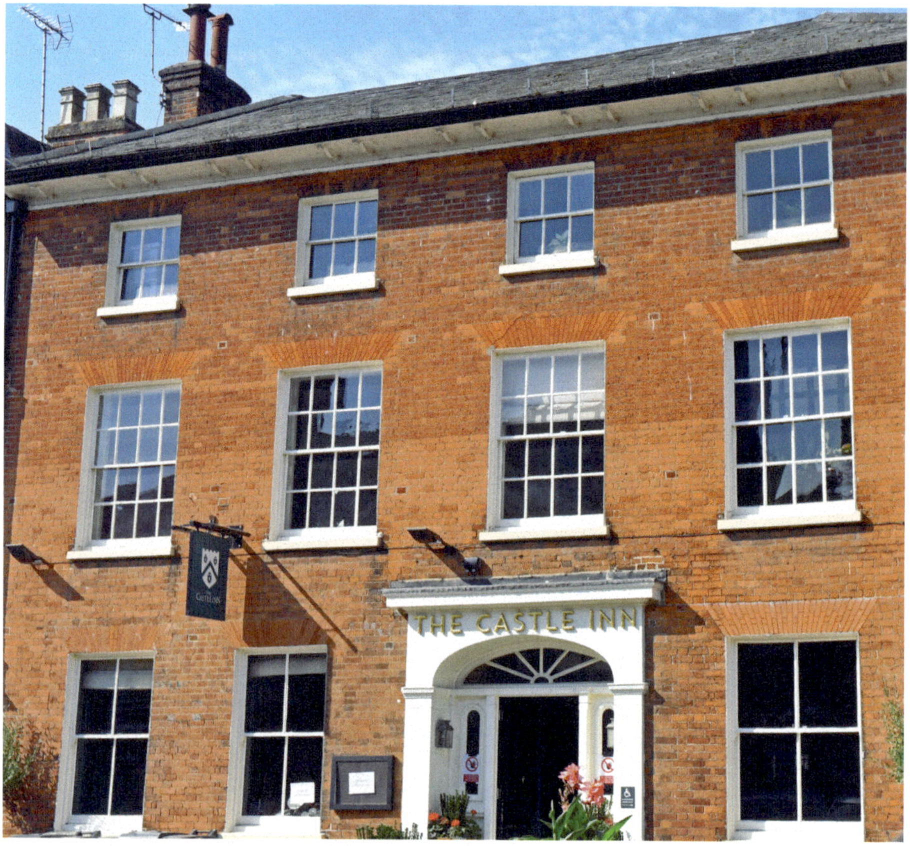

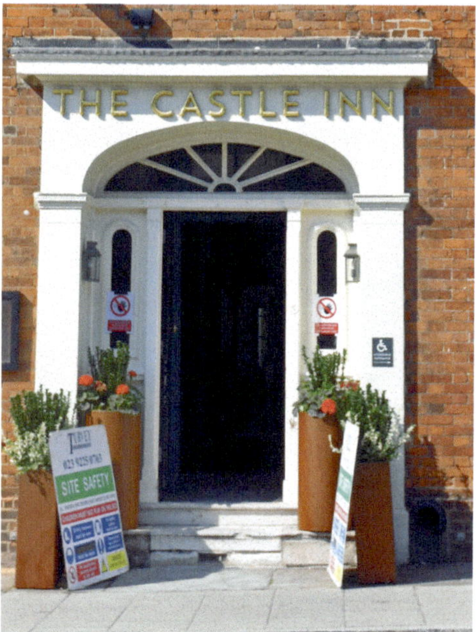

Above: The three-storey, brick, asymmetrical former Castle Inn on Castle Street has an off-centre doorcase and a range of Georgian windows of different sizes.

Left: The off-centre doorway of the former Castle Inn on Castle Street has a double door, round-headed side lights, a fanlight, and a stone doorcase that incorporates an elliptical arch.

The larger first-floor windows are wider and taller than the others with sixteen panes, while the top-floor windows are narrower and lower with only six panes. The former inn now acts as a business premises. During the Second World War it was a Red Cross station.

43. The Narrow House and Shop, West Street, Nineteenth Century

The narrow brick house and shop on West Street dates from the nineteenth century and features a ground-floor shop with two floors overhead. The shopfront stretches across the front and features plain side columns at both ends with an overhead moulded fascia, between which is a bowed display window, one of a

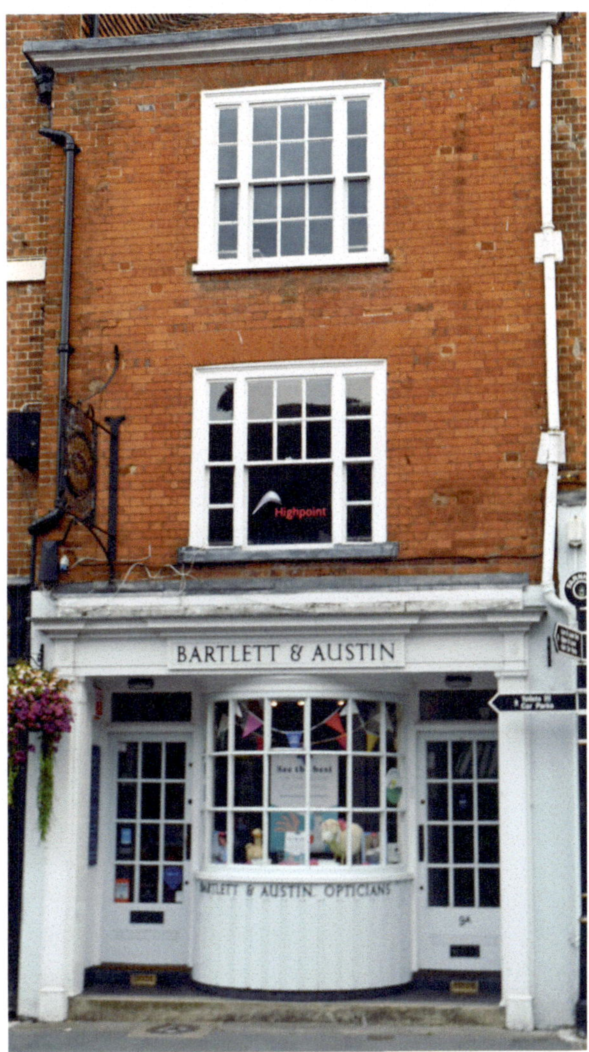

The stylish, narrow, brick house and shop on West Street features a bow-fronted shopfront with two floors and Palladian windows overhead.

number of bow-fronted shopfronts in Farnham, with a doorway on either side. The Georgian-styled bowed display window has square panes, matching doors on either side and seems to be a recent insertion. The doors have glazed panels and rectangular fanlights. One provides access to the shop and the other gives access to the accommodation on the upper floors. The windows on the two upper floors are Palladian in style with a wide central sliding sash flanked on either side by a narrower sash – both with Georgian-style glazing. Overhead, the hipped slated roof has projecting eaves.

44. Two-storey Rendered Shops, Downing Street, Nineteenth Century

The pair of double-storey arcaded shops on Downing Street with matching picturesque elevations date from around 1855, and were sympathetically restored during the 1950s. The elevation is divided into four bays, two wide and two narrow, separated by plain pilaster. The two central bays have a similar arched

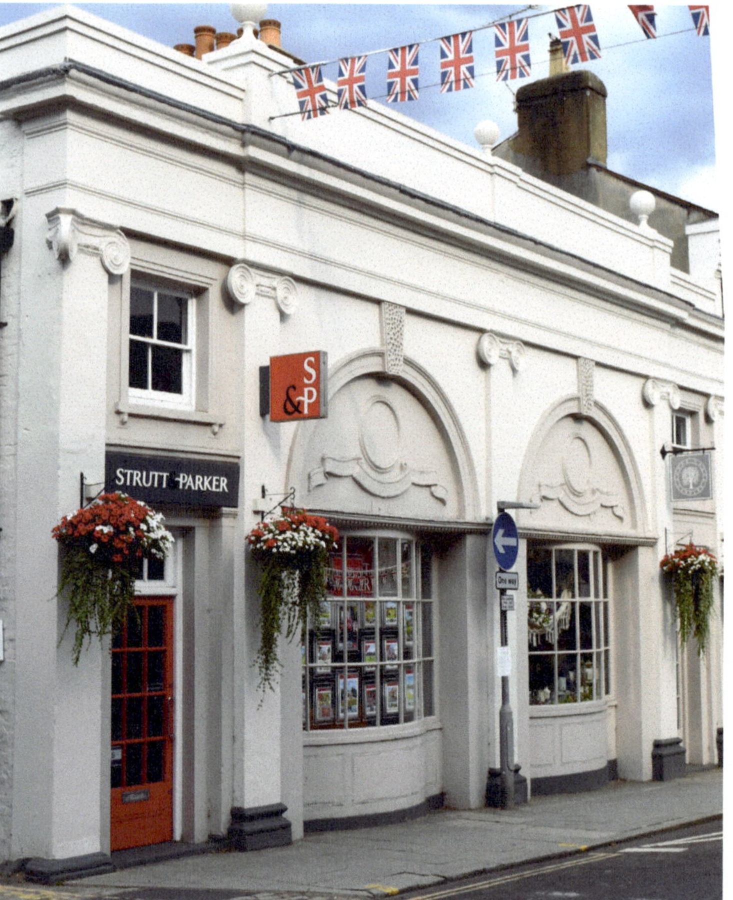

The complex picturesque elevation of the arcaded shops on Downing Street has Georgian-style bow windows, arches, plain pilasters, and small Georgian windows, as well as a moulded fascia and parapet.

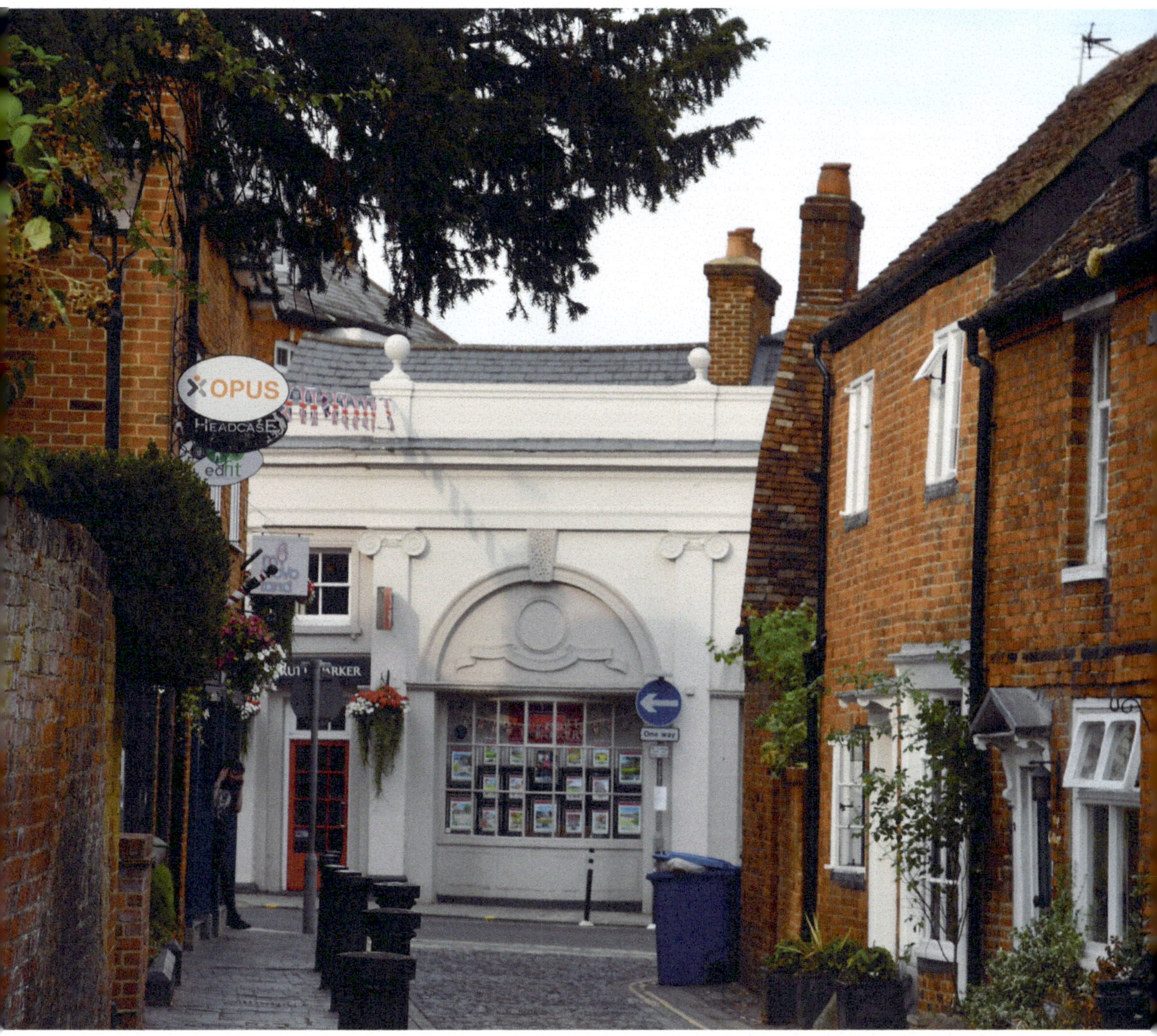

The arcaded shops on Downing Street offer an impressive closing vista to Upper Church Lane.

shop window with overhead semicircular arches each with decorative panels, moulded surrounds and wedge-shaped keystones. The flat-headed display windows are bow shaped with small Georgian panes and a plain rendered base. The narrow bays at either end have a doorway and a small casement window on the upper level. The doors have Georgian-style glazed panels and a rectangular fan sash, while the first-floor windows are divided into four panes. Over the double arch a moulded fascia stretches across the building, from side to side, above which is a moulded cornice and a stepped parapet, with three ball-topped obelisks. In the past the building held a fishmonger and a coffee tavern.

45. Former Stable, Castle Street, Nineteenth Century

The narrow two-storey building acted as a stable block to the adjoining Castle Inn on Castle Street (see No. 42, p. 77) during the nineteenth century, which was subsequently converted to commercial use. Today the attractive brick building features three interesting arches and a brick pediment. The ground floor has a cambered entrance door to one side and a wider but slightly lower segmental arched display windows with a pattern of small Georgian glazing bars on the other side. The first floor has a prominent elliptical window in a central position with a pattern of radial glazing bars. Overhead, the plain brick parapet has a stone stringcourse and a stone coping.

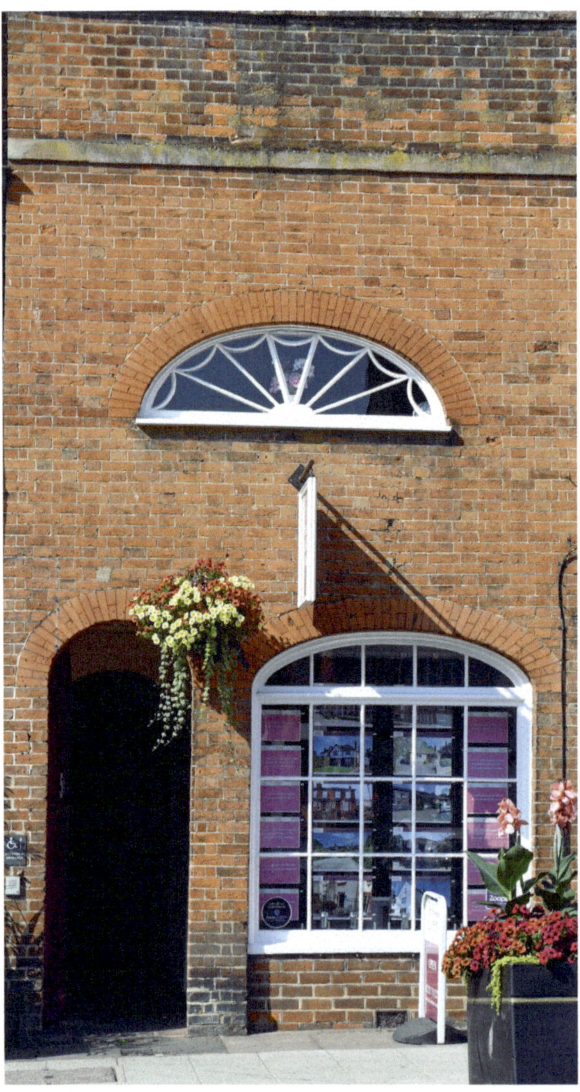

The impressive brick-built former stable building on Castle Street has a sequence of arched openings, including the first-floor elliptical window with its a distinctive pattern of radiating glazing bars and a plain-brick pediment.

46. St Andrew's School, Upper Church Lane, 1860

St Andrew's School on Upper Church Lane represents one of the earliest Gothic Revival buildings to appear in Farnham. This incorporated the form of medieval church building technology, including masonry walling, steep roofs, gables, pointed windows and door openings and a stone image of St Andrew. Work began on the church in 1860 under the direction of the architect John Colston, and subsequently experienced considerable amendments and extensions. Today the initial historic block features a long stone building with a central gable flanked by two smaller gables and a tall, tiled roof and corner buttresses. The tall central gable has a pair of side-by-side Gothic-style windows with tracery and a small round window near

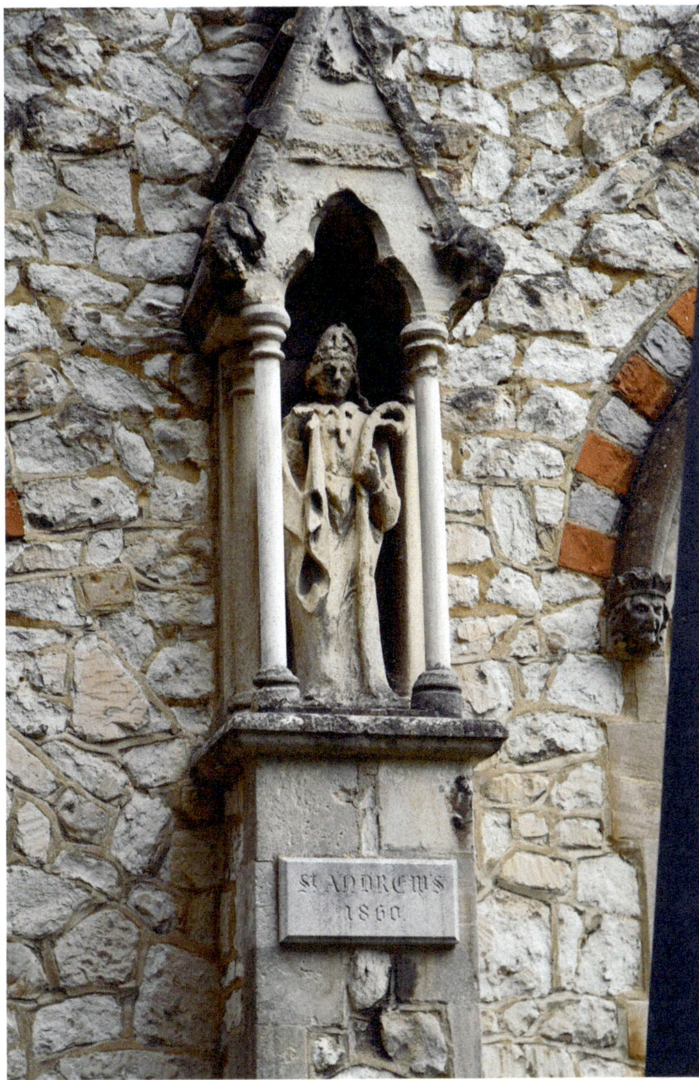

The image of St Andrew was incorporated into the stone elevation of St Andrew's School on Upper Church Lane in 1860.

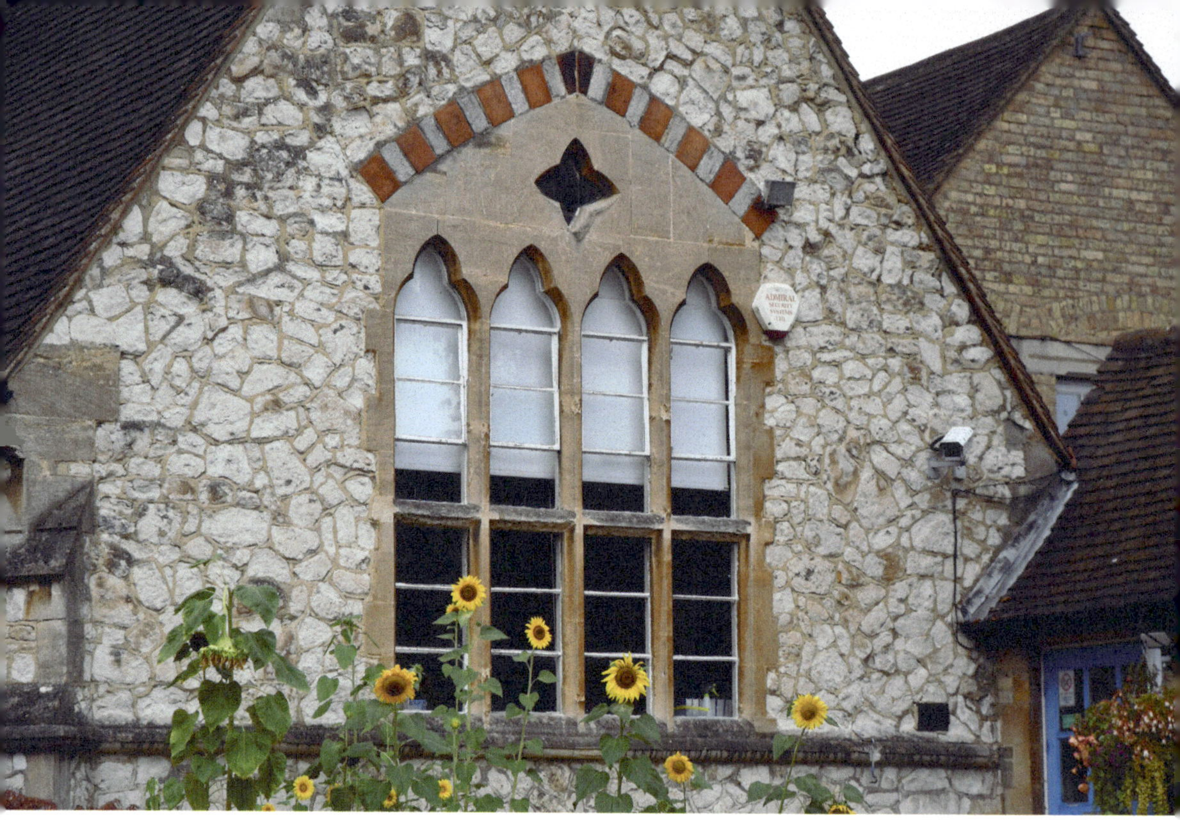

Above: The gable of St Andrew's School on Upper Church Lane has an impressive cut stone east window with trefoil heads.

Below: The former schoolmaster house, like St Andrew's School, on Upper Church Lane, features elements of the Gothic Revival style.

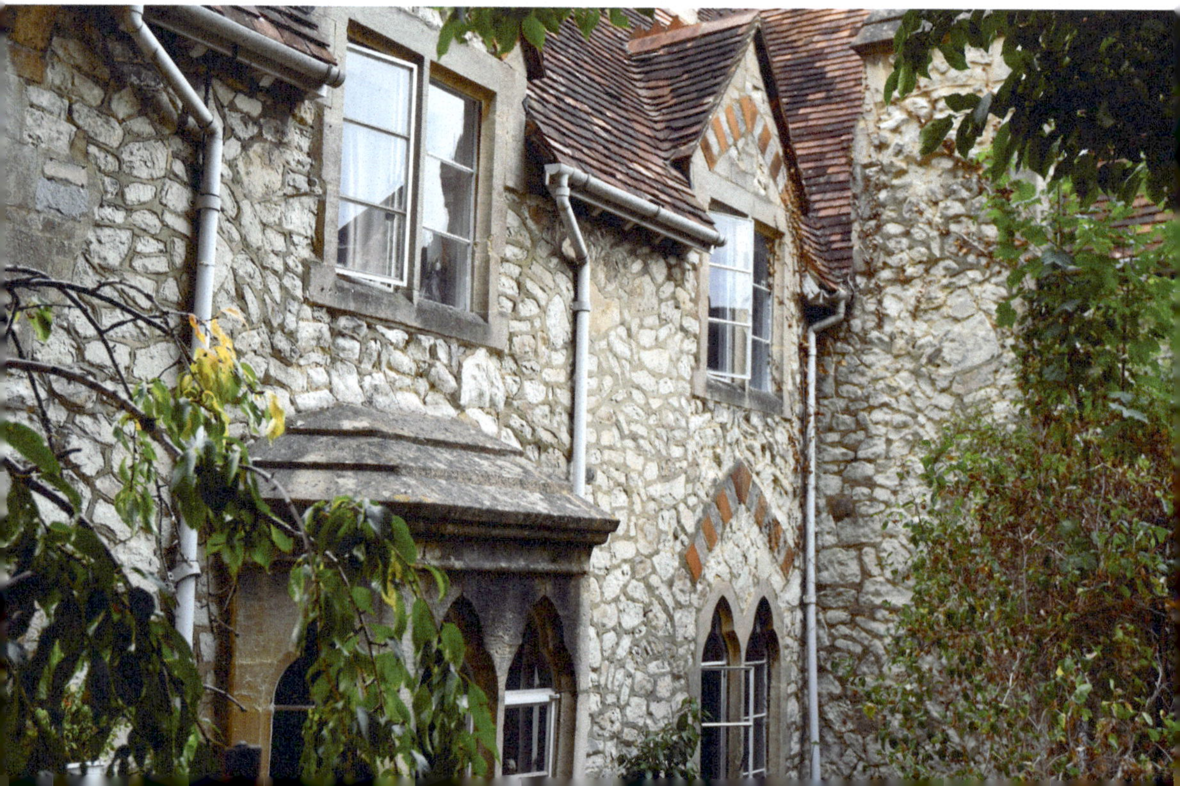

the apex. The side gables are lower and each has a single window with tracery. In addition, the elevation has pairs of pointed windows set between the gabbles. The high pointed east gable has a large single mullion and transom window with four slim lights, each with a trefoil head and an overhead relieving arch. Beside the school is the similar-styled former schoolmaster's house that also dates from around 1860 and displays similar Gothic Revival features including stone walling, gables, tiled roofs, tall masonry chimneys, and casement windows.

47. Farnham Adult Learning Centre, West Street, 1872

The two-storey Farnham Adult Education Centre on West Street dates from the nineteenth century and consists of four bays: two slightly projecting end gabled bays and two level-headed middle bays. The east bay was built first (1872) in grey

The two-storey, brick, Jacobin-style Farnham Adult Learning Centre in West Street has projecting gabled side bays and cut stone transom and mullion windows.

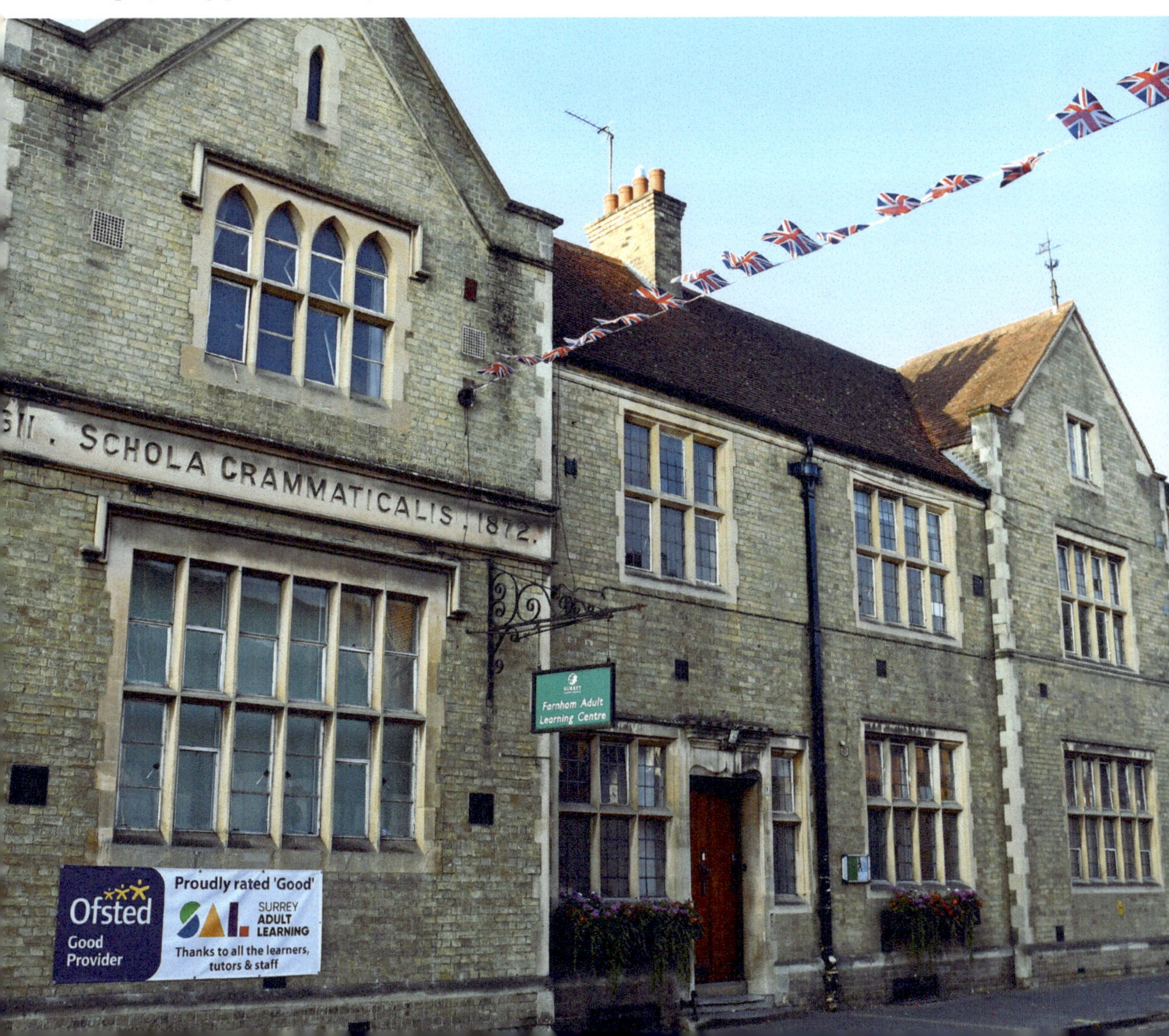

brick as a grammar school with 'SCOLA GRAMMATICALUS 1872' inscribed on the first-floor stringcourse. The architect was Paxton Watson and he chose a Jacobin Revival style – a style of architecture modelled on the that of the Jacobin period. Following the initial stage the remaining three bays were built in 1895 in a similar Jacobin Revival form. The block was partially built on the site of an eighteenth house. It was initially used as an art school and in recent years became the Farnham Adult Learning Centre.

The initial east bay has stone quoins and a transom and mullion window with cut stone dressing on each level. The ground-floor window is the widest with

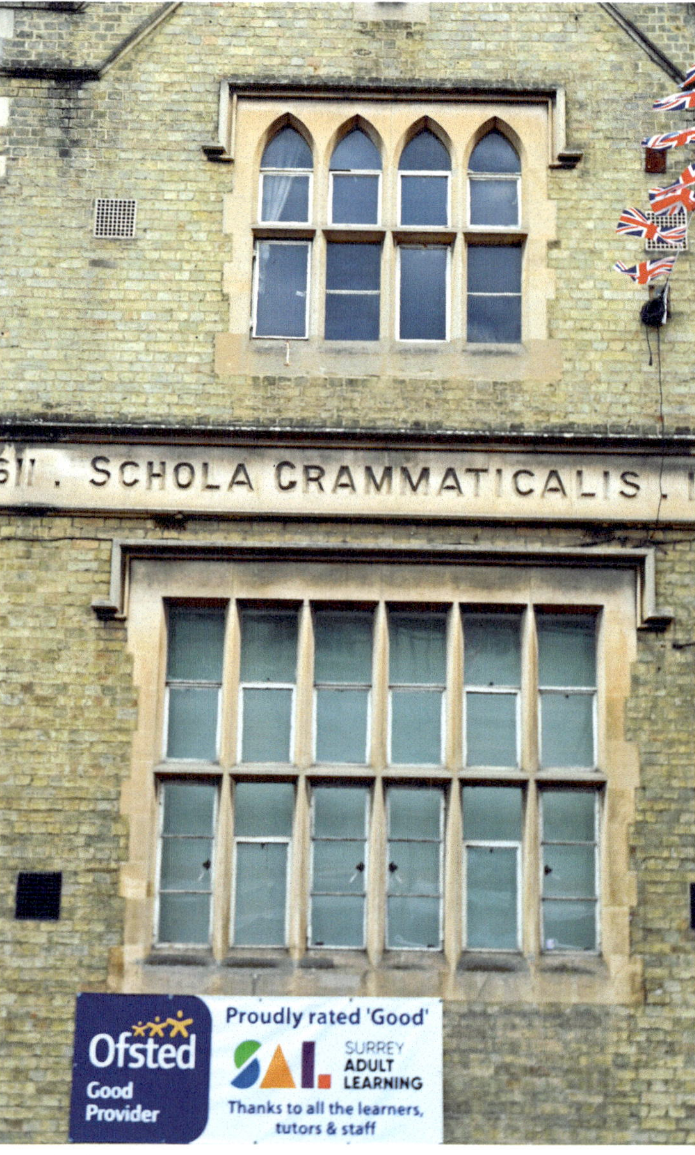

The gable east bay of the Farnham Adult Learning Centre has transom and mullion windows, an inscribed school sign, and cut stone dressing.

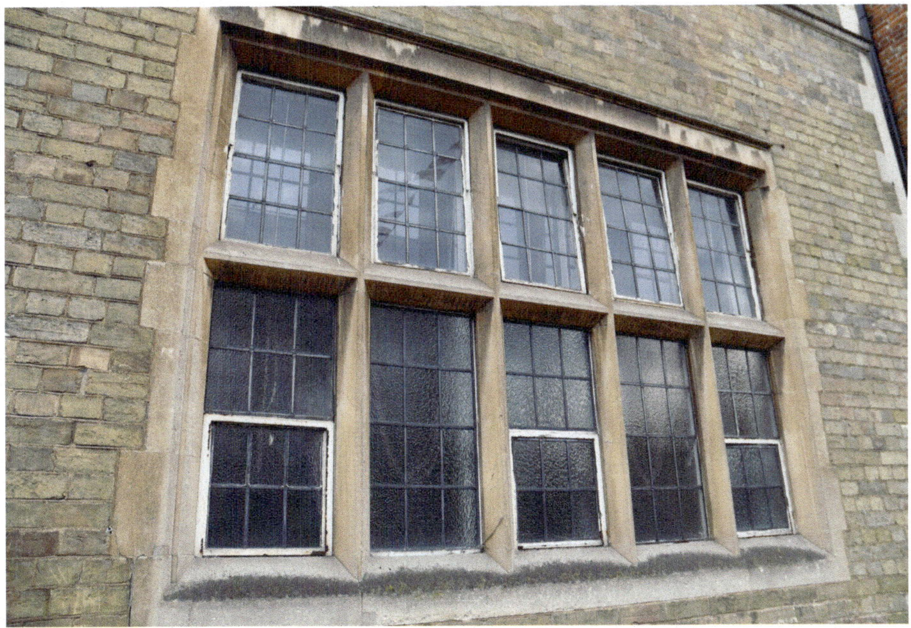

The ground-level transom and mullion windows of the Farnham Adult Learning Centre on West Street are divided into panes by stone uprights, a cross piece and surrounds.

twelve panes, while the narrower upper-level window has eight panes. The panes of the upper window have pointed heads. There is also a slim lancet window in the apex of the gable. To the right of the ground-level window is a metal ornamental bracket with a hanging sign declaring the Farnham Adult Learning Centre. The opposite west side gabled bay is similar in form, although the transom and mullion windows are narrower. The ground-floor window has ten bays and the upper level has eight. Additionally, the upper window lacks the pointed heads of the eastern bay and overhead the apex has a small two-pane window. The two centre bays also have stone-framed transom and mullion windows on both floors in addition to a doorcase to one side. This has an off-centre sheeted door set into a transom and mullion opening with cut stone framing.

48. NatWest, The Borough, 1865

The NatWest bank on The Borough was modelled on an Italianate style and offers a dramatic closing vista to Castle Street. The bank was completed in two stages under the architect Horace Cheston, although at different times. The east side dates from 1865 and the west side 1904. Despite the symmetrical arrangement of the three-storey building, the elevation to the street is visually complex, with rendering on the ground-floor level, painted brickwork on the upper floors, and a mixed arrangement of windows and doors, which although vertically aligned and

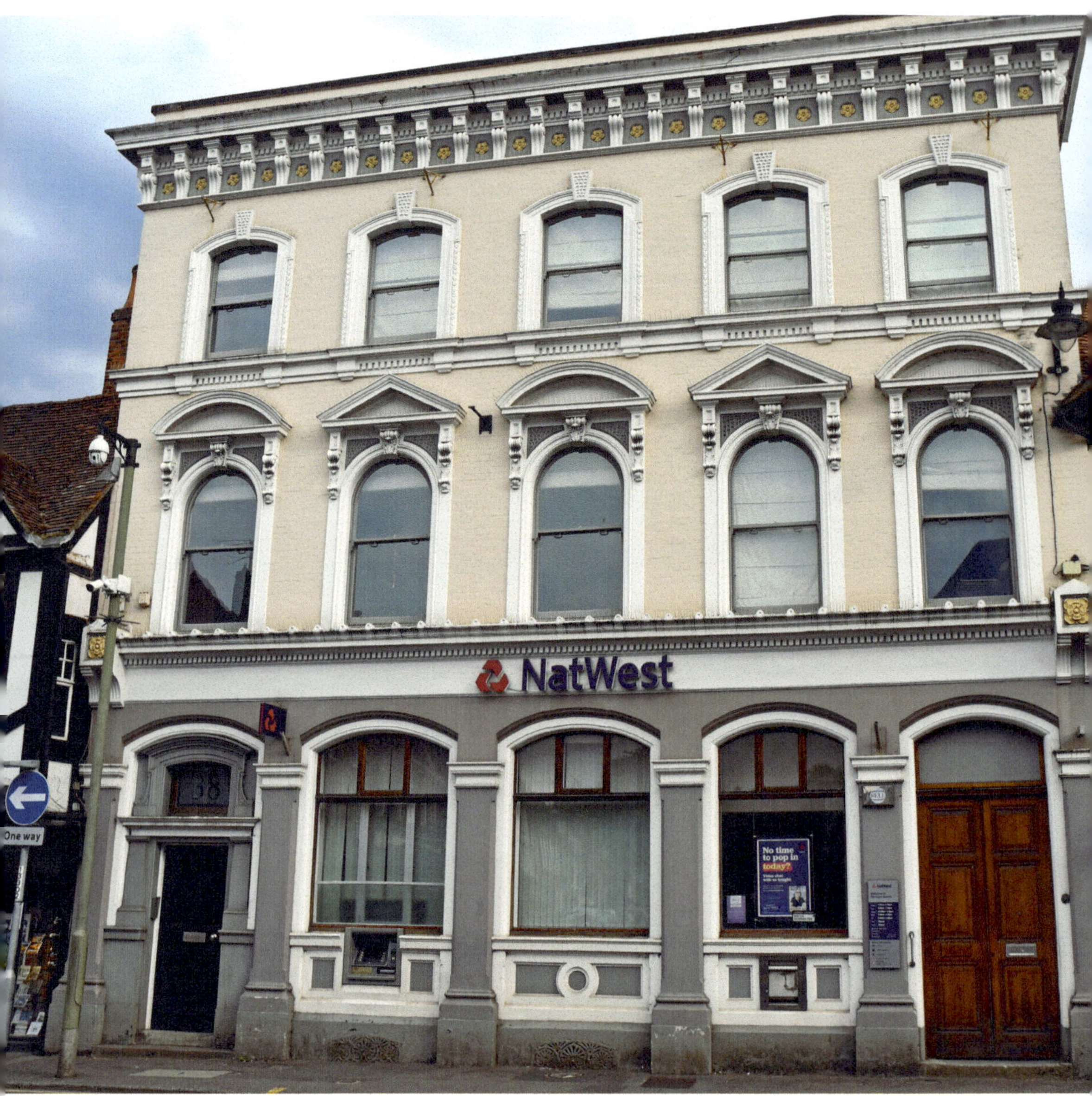

The rendered, three-storey, Italianate-style NatWest bank on The Borough has a range of curve-headed doors and window openings, and offers an impressive closing vista to Castle Street.

uniformly distributed across the front, differ in scale and form. The ground level has a sequence of five bays extending across the front containing three windows and a doorway at either end. Above the cambered arches is a plain fascia, with a modest bank sign that extends across the elevation. The five windows of the first floor are the most elaborate. The have sliding sashes that lack glazing bars, arched

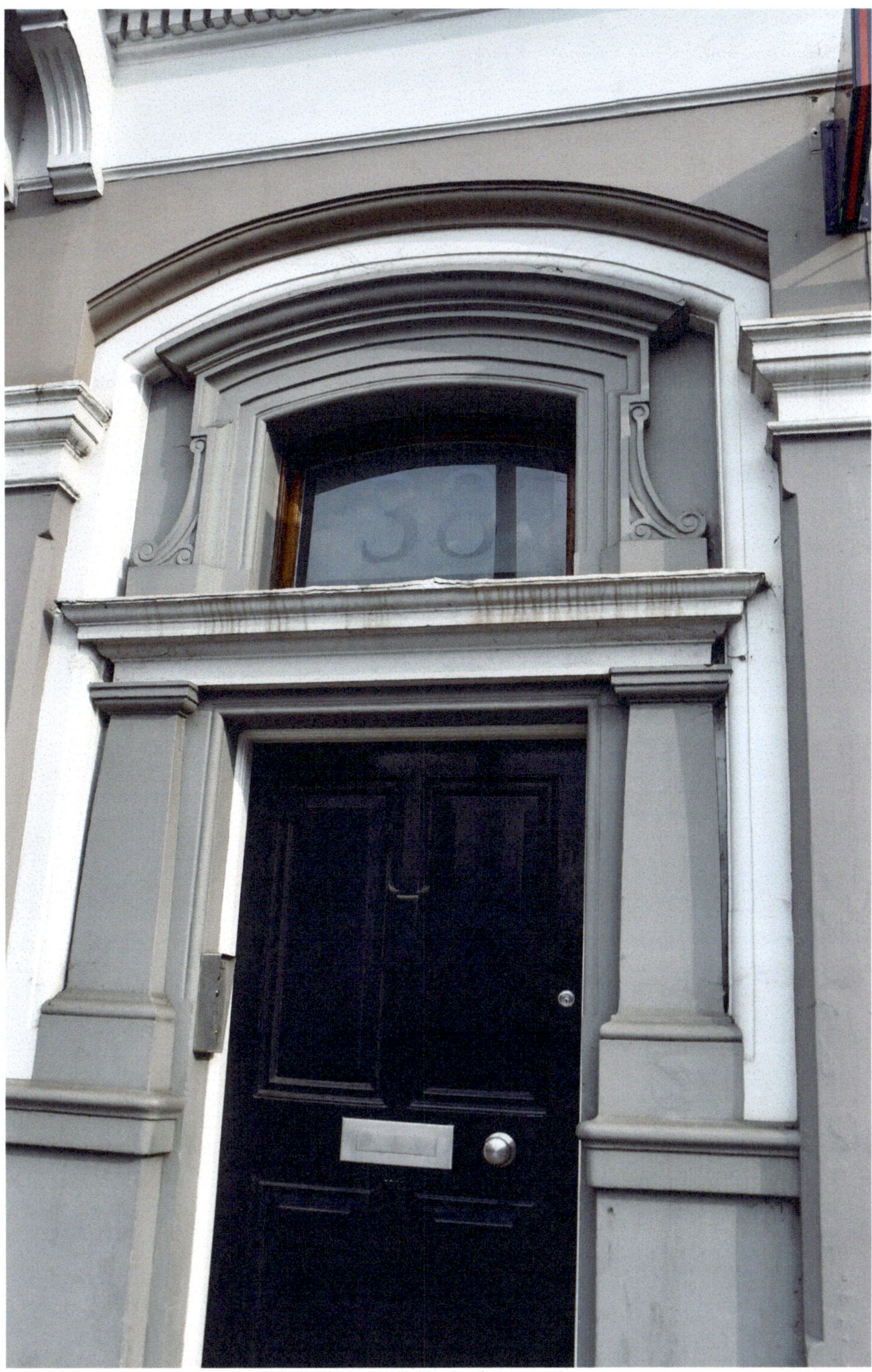

The elaborate doorway of the NatWest bank on The Borough has a panelled door, plain side columns, a cambered fanlight, and upper-level moulded surrounds.

heads, moulded surrounds, elaborate side brackets, keystones and triangular pediments. The second-floor windows are similar with sliding sashes, no glazing bars, cambered heads, moulded surrounds, and wedge-shaped keystones. At the base of these windows the sills are incorporated into a decorated stringcourse that extends across the elevation. Above the windows the tiled roof is mainly screened by the painted brick parapet that includes a moulded cornice and projecting eaves brackets and decorated panels.

49. Lloyds Bank, Castle Street, 1931

Although dating from 1931, the Lloyds Bank building on Castle Street was built in a bold Georgian Revival style by the architects Guy, Dawber and Wilson, on the site of the former Knight brothers' Farnham Bank. The three-bay symmetrical brick building is two storeys high with a prominent triangular pediment at roof level, a tiled roof and sliding Georgian windows with square multi-pane glazing. The central bay steps forward from the side bays and features the entrance door, ground- and first-floor windows and pediment. The ground level centrally positioned double-leaf entrance door has a moulded surround, a rectangular fanlight with a metal radial inset, and a wedge-shaped

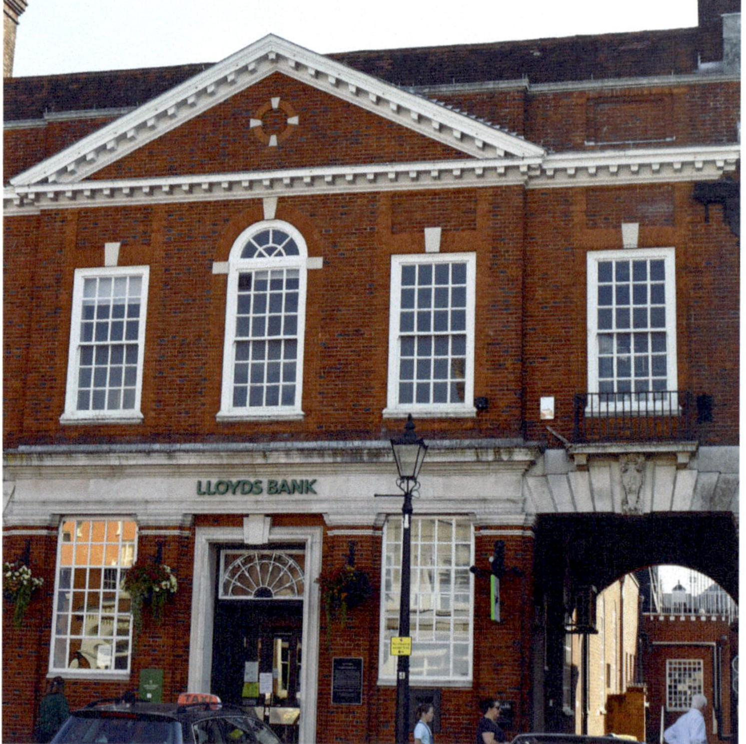

The Georgian Revival-style, three-bay Lloyds Bank on Castle Street is two storeys high with multiple-pane windows and a prominent triangular roofline pediment.

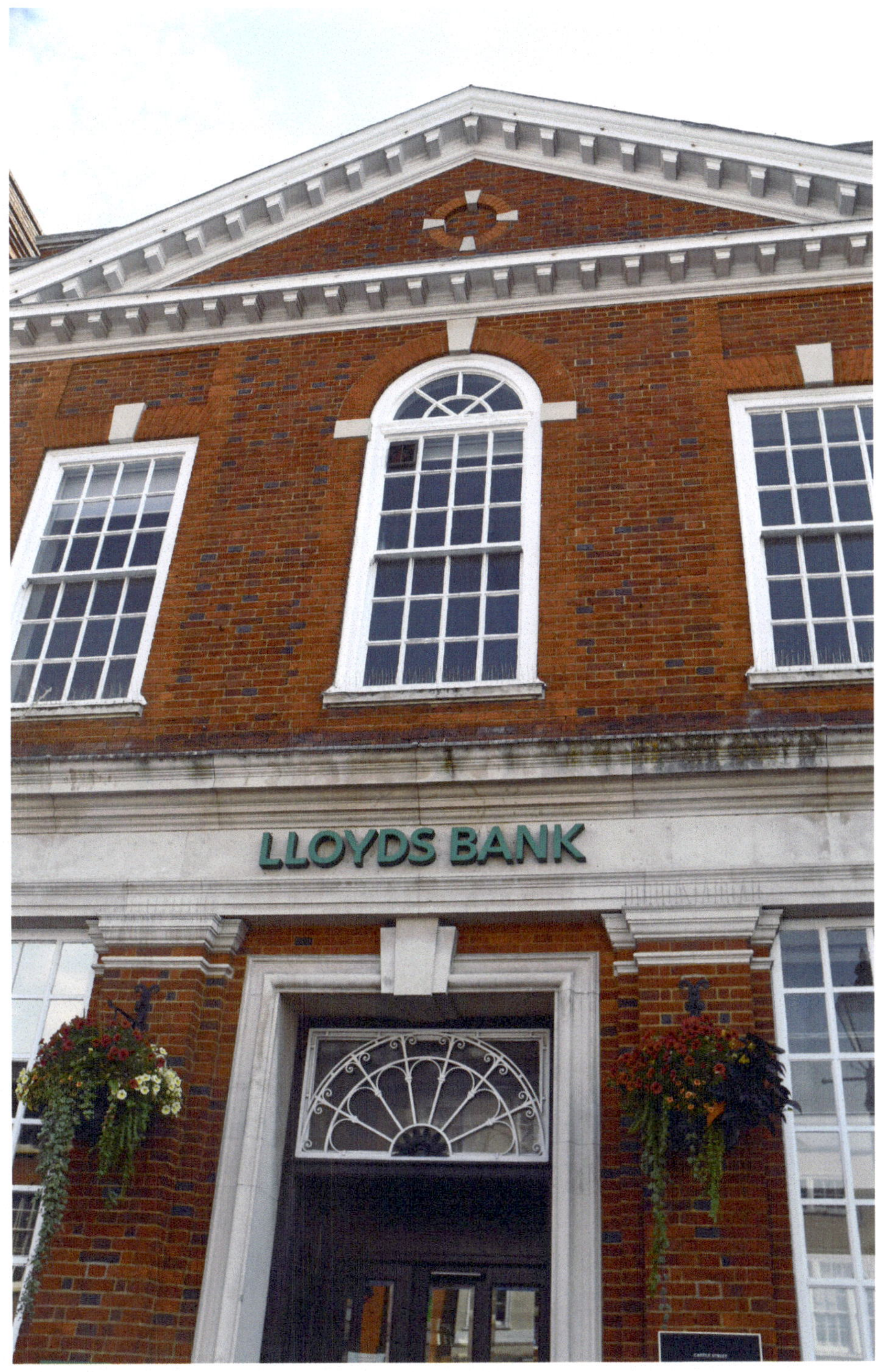

The vertically aligned entrance door, fanlight and round-headed window of Lloyds Bank on Castle Street emphasise the central approach to the building.

keystone at the head. This is flanked on both sides by a single Georgian sliding window with multiple square panes and a wide cut stone moulded fascia overhead. The first floor has three windows evenly spaced across the bay. The two side windows are smaller than those on the ground level, but with plain surrounds and a wedge-shaped keystone. The central window is similar, but with a rounded head. Overhead, the wide triangular pediment stretches across the central bay and has moulded base and edges and a round panel in the apex. The narrow left-hand side bay has similar windows to those on the central bay – one on each level with a cut stone rusticated keystone lintel over the upper sash. The bay on the opposite side of the elevation is similarly arranged, except for the coach arch at ground level. This extends across the full width of the bay and also has a cut stone keystone lintel. The brick parapet at roof level flanks the sides of the pediment and has recessed panels both above and below the moulded stone cornice.

50. Town Hall Buildings, Castle Street/The Borough, 1932

The double-storey brick Town Hall Buildings at the corner of Castle Street and The Borough is an imposing and complex block that dates from 1932 and was built on the site of the former wooden-framed market house that had been demolished in 1866. The building was designed in a Georgian Revival style by the architects Falkner, Aylwin and Bensdlyn and was completed with a single bay facing onto Castle Street and three side bays facing The Borough. The Castle Street ground-level bay features an arcade of five arched windows, with a door at one end and an open arch at the other end. These semicircular archways feature a mixture of plain brick and stone surrounds. The first-floor level has standard Georgian windows with cambered heads that stretch uniformly across the elevation, in addition to a stone stringcourse that mark the two floor levels. The projecting eaves of the building is particularly notable as it extends outwards in a curve with a decorated soffit. One of the most significant features of the Town Hall building is the magnificent cupola and weathervane positioned on the apex of the tiled roof. This includes a splayed copper base that incorporates a clockface, an arched and columned lantern, a copper dome, and a weathervane, mounted by a model of Drake's ship, the *Golden Hind*, in full sail. The former gas lamp that stands prominently in front of the Castle Street elevation is one of a range of slim metal street lamps, with glazed lamps and access bars that extend along Castle street and represent an important nineteenth-century streetscape element of the town. The three-bay Borough elevation of the Town Hall is similar in form to Castle Street, with the addition of an open arcade, rounded columns, flat and moulded arches, as well as Georgian and dormer windows.

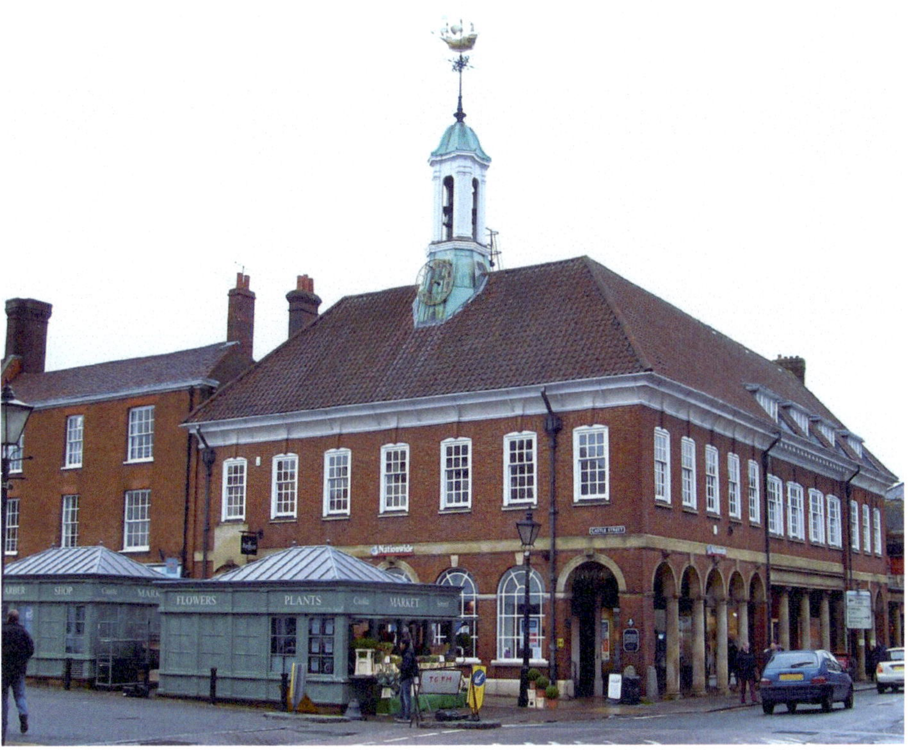

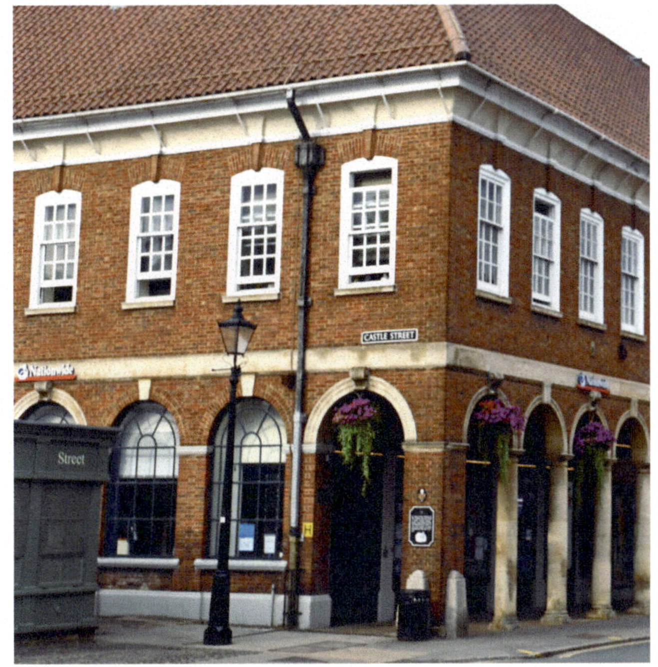

Above: Farnham Town Hall Buildings, 2014. (© Len Williams, CC BY-SA 2.0)

Right: The brick Farnham Town Hall Buildings are strategically positioned at the corner of Castle Street and The Borough and feature arches, Georgian windows, projecting eaves, and a tiled roof.

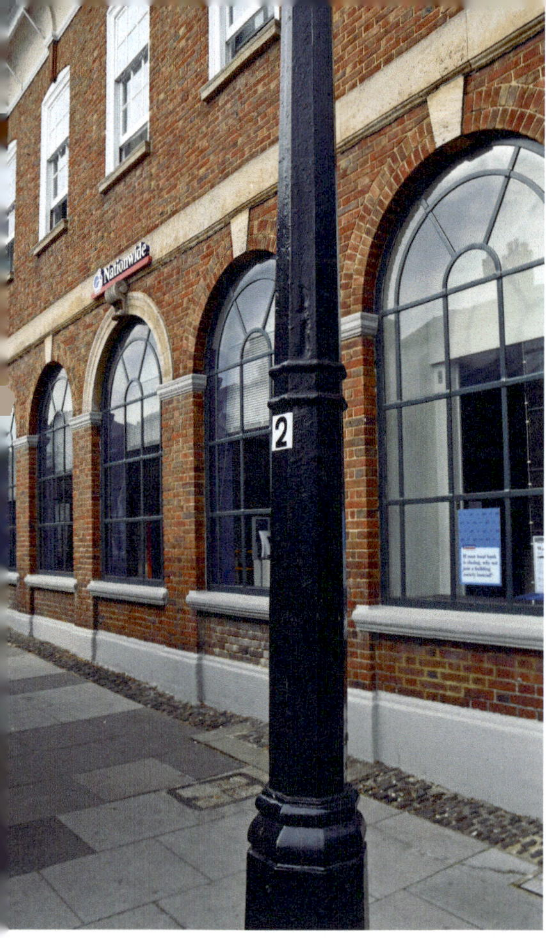

Left: The Castle Street front of the Town Hall Buildings features brick arches, curved windows, Georgian windows, projecting eaves, and a lamp standard immediately in front of the building.

Below: The projecting, rendered, coved and decorated eaves are a notable feature.

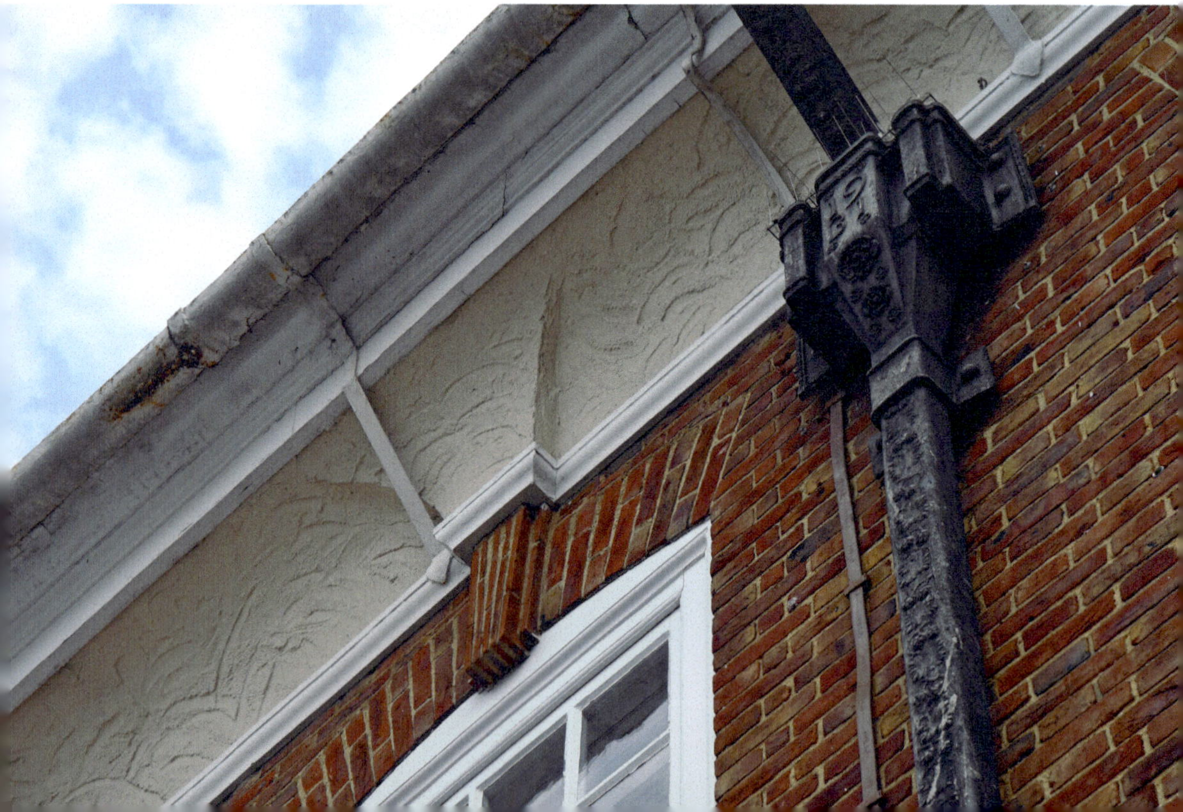

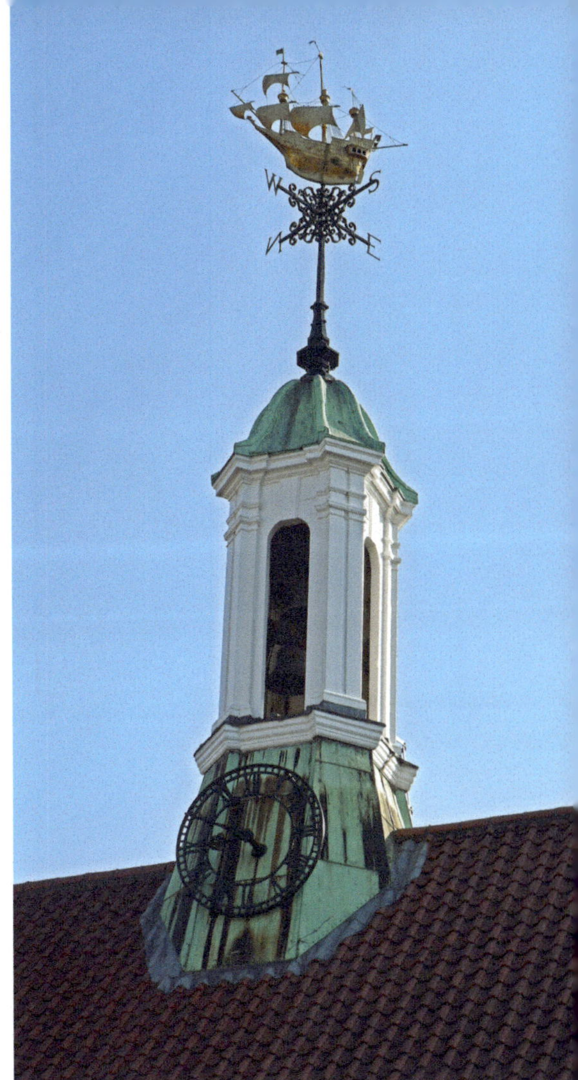

The cupola on the ridge of the tiled
roof includes a base, clock face, lantern,
weathervane and a model of a ship – the
Golden Hind.

The nineteenth-century former gas lamp at the
front of the Town Hall Buildings has a slim
metal standard, a glazed lamp and a decorated
access bar.

Also by the Author

Exploring Georgian Dublin (2008)
Exploring Ireland's Historic Towns (2010)
Exploring Irish Castles (2011)
Exploring Celtic Ireland (2011)
Exploring Georgian Limerick (2012)
Georgian Bath (2012)
Georgian London: The West End (2012)
The Georgian Town House (2013)
Edinburgh New Town, co-authored by Carley, Dalziel and Laird (2015)
Dublin in 50 Buildings (2017)
Bath in 50 Buildings (2018)
Dublin Pubs (2018)
Limerick in 50 Buildings (2019)
Kilkenny: City of Heritage (2019)
Whitehaven in 50 Buildings (2020)
Wexford Town of Heritage (2023)

Printed and bound by CPI Group (UK) Ltd, Croydon, CR0 4YY

05/03/2026

02065465-0005